GHOSTS OF
LEAVENWORTH
AND THE
CASCADE FOOTHILLS

GHOSTS OF
LEAVENWORTH
AND THE
CASCADE FOOTHILLS

DEBORAH CUYLE

HAUNTED
America

Published by Haunted America
A Division of The History Press
Charleston, SC
www.historypress.net

Front cover: Courtesy of Sue Cragun of City of Leavenworth.

First published 2017

ISBN 9781540226464

Library of Congress Control Number: 2017940950

Notice: The information in this book is true and complete to the best of our knowledge. It is offered without guarantee on the part of the author or The History Press. The author and The History Press disclaim all liability in connection with the use of this book.

DEDICATION

Some things have to be believed to be seen.
—Ralph Hodgson

All a skeptic is, is someone who hasn't had an experience yet.
—Jason Hawes

I've always believed in the paranormal. I mean, there is a paranormal, there are
spirits and there are ghosts. Anybody who doesn't believe there are, is being silly,
because what runs this vessel is energy. And you can't kill energy, you can only
displace it. It has to go somewhere. So there are spirits, as we call them,—of
course there are.
—Eric Roberts, Celebrity Ghost Stories

"Some people can't see the color red. That doesn't mean it isn't there," she replied.
—Sue Grafton, M Is for Malice

This book is dedicated to everyone who loves Leavenworth and Washington State as much as I do and to all the people out there who are curious about the afterlife. Upon investigating Leavenworth, I was surprised to find more peaceful types of spirit(s) roaming about. Even the stories I collected from locals and patrons always suggested a kind and comforting (although sometimes mischievous) type of ghost, instead of scary or intimidating spirits. My intuition was credited by the fact that many times when talking to business owners, employees and locals, they would suggest, "Oh, we are not haunted...but we *do* have ghosts!" in a cheery, almost excited voice, and there actually is a difference between the two.

That being the case, I immersed myself into massive amounts of research about the early pioneers who worked so hard to create the town (then called Icicle) and who believed without a doubt that someday Leavenworth would be magnificent.

Even after the repeated, tragic and devastating fires that torched their town to the ground, they progressively rebuilt their stores and houses and barns without a single thought of ever leaving—still bragging about how lovely their town is, even as they cleaned the soot from their clothes.

As I investigated and learned more about these pioneers, it made more sense. The spirits of the wonderful people who built Leavenworth probably have no desire to ever leave it. The local stories I heard were mostly about items being moved along with the slightest sense of being watched, as if the ghosts were saying, "Here I am! When this was my business, I kept the register over here—and now wouldn't those things look better over by the window? I dare say, it's going to be a busy day!"

The unanimous thought was that the ghosts of Leavenworth are just kindly, giving helpful advice or offering a reassuring nudge in the right direction for the buildings' new proprietors. Nowhere in Leavenworth did I experience a frightening or eerie spirit presence.

Being a NDE (near death experience) survivor, I am probably a little more open-minded than most people. That tends to happen. Perhaps someday science can prove what really happens to us after we die—the eternal mystery—but until then it is all just speculation. Religion and science may someday agree, and maybe not. I see both sides of the debate. Too many unexplained things happen to each of us to not entertain the idea of ghosts and the spirit world. I read somewhere that God or spirits do give us signs when we ask for them, but we as humans are too busy or too close-minded to see them for what they are.

I also dedicate this book to my incredible son, Dane Brown, who has always been my best friend and cohort in a passion for writing. To my wonderful Middy, who never complains when I am writing nonstop even though a yummy dinner and couple cold cocktails are waiting for me to share with him. My love also goes to all my spiritual BFFs who have joined me in a little ghost hunting and support my paranormal research and beliefs. An open mind is an open door.

And last but not least, to my incredible and loving mom, Roxine, who always believed I could do whatever I set my mind out to do.

I often get asked many questions about ghosts, my NDE, the paranormal world, receiving messages from the other side. I have had so many experiences it is hard for me to narrow it down to just one when discussing them with people. I look forward to having many more.

—Deborah Cuyle-Fletcher

CONTENTS

CONTENTS

PREFACE

This book project is for my love of pioneers, local history and old buildings. I love all the lore and legends, ghosts and spirit stories people have told me over the years. It is fun to walk the same streets today, the same ones early settlers once walked, and think of how it was back in the old days. History is full of people who haunt us, who want to be recognized and never forgotten for what they did, what they created, what they offered. This book is about those fascinating spirits—the spirited people who made Leavenworth and the Cascade Foothills what they are today.

Deep snow on Front Street near the Palm Billiard Hall, which was opened by Harry Moore in the summer of 1909. Wenatchee Steam Laundry would drop off and pick up clients' laundry at the Palm. J.D. Wheeler photo. *Courtesy of Skykomish Historical Society.*

During the 1920 and '30s, it was popular to enjoy "tin pants sledding" a process of applying paraffin to the seat of the pants and sliding down a snow field. *Photo commissioned by the Department of Commerce and Economic Development courtesy of Washington State Archives, Preparing tin pants, 1920, State Library Photograph Collection, 1851–1990, Washington State Digital Archives, www. digitalarchives.wa.gov.*

In 1930, a group of visitors on the Paradise Glacier at Mount Rainier National Park watching as individuals slide down on "tin pants." *Courtesy of Washington State Digital Archives, "Tin pants sledding at Mount Rainier," 1930–1935, Lindsley, L.D., Washington State Library Photograph Collection, 1851–1990.*

The stories here have been told to me by locals or dredged out of old newspapers and some names in the stories have been changed to protect the innocent (or guilty?), but all told out of fun for the love of history and lore.

The book is not intended to be a nonfiction project, and even after thousands of hours hunched over reading and researching, I still found conflicting dates and inconsistent historic details—so please take it for what it is. I tried hard to be as accurate with names, dates and details as much as possible. This is mostly a book full of tales of mischievous ghosts and the interesting history of the town. Enjoy!

ACKNOWLEDGEMENTS

M y gratitude goes out to all the wonderful people who work for Arcadia Publishing and The History Press. Without their extreme amount of kindness, knowledge and patience, I am sure many books would never even make it to print. I also want to thank the numerous hardworking volunteers at local historical societies and museums as they spend countless hours documenting newspaper clippings, scanning photographs and finding maps and a million other things so that history is well preserved for future generations to enjoy.

As for this project, I would like to thank Jessica Stoller of the Leavenworth Chamber; Mike Buscher of Library of Congress; Mary Schaff of the Washington State Library; Bob Kelly of the Skykomish Historical Society; Glenn Brautaset, deputy of Chief Operations Chelan County Fire District 3; the *Leavenworth Echo* newspaper; Sandy Owens-Carmody of the Tumwater Inn; Sandy of Temptations Boutique in Cashmere; and many other contributors. If I have forgotten to list you here, please forgive me!

And a big thank-you to all the many friendly neighbors and locals who told me their stories in order for me to share them with you. (Some names of people and places have been changed to protect their identity. I hope readers will respect people's privacy and not disrupt any businesses or trespass on personal property.)

INTRODUCTION

The miracle town of Leavenworth, Washington, is known for its beautiful Bavarian theme, wonderful shopping and restaurants, friendly people and redesigned historical buildings. Old architectural designs from the early 1900s nestled in between a few modern ones are packed tight on Front Street, and those that survived the tragic fires remain almost frozen in time. When Leavenworth had to reinvent itself or else become another ghost town, the townspeople opted to undergo the daunting task and make the switch to a Bavarian theme to create a unique, one-of-a-kind town.

People visit from all over to enjoy a bustling day of shopping, great food, fabulous boutiques, live music and local art, as well as partaking in the many festivals, events and parades. For a small town, it holds its own when it comes to creating a unique and thriving atmosphere for millions of visitors to enjoy year-round.

When strolling the sidewalks today, moving in and out of the wonderful shops, please imagine what life must have been like back then—the old times of horse carriages, hardworking hotel and restaurant proprietors, muddy dirt streets, the building of the railroads and the mining of gold.

In 1901, the population of Leavenworth was approximately 450 people; it bumped up to around 1,400 in 1908. Automobiles were a rare luxury in Leavenworth at the time. In 1910, there was only one noted auto owned and operated in town. In 1912, a whopping five people had their own cars. Later, in 1914, over forty cars cruised the streets of Leavenworth.

Good roads were a huge problem to residents, and in 1914, the Washington State Automobile Association was formed to promote the development of good roads for the public. *Courtesy of Washington State Digital Archives, 1927, Autos on the road to Bothell, State Library Photograph Collection, item # AR-07809001-ph000092.*

When they say Leavenworth is a "miracle town," one often thinks of the town's transformation to save itself in the '60s from a near extinction to the infamous Bavarian village everyone loves and enjoys today. This particular transformation has been very well documented by several authors.

Yet another sometimes overlooked miracle is how many times in the early years the town suffered substantial loss from fires and continued to rebuild itself. How these citizens rebuilt their town over and over again without falter or succumbing to discouragement is truly miraculous—what a fantastic and adventurous group of people.

Early Leavenworth was quite progressive. In the 1900s, two of the biggest employers were the Great Northern Railroad and Lamb-Davis Lumber Company. Great Northern employed about three hundred to four hundred men at a time with a payroll of about $30,000 per month. Lamb-Davis employed around two to three hundred, and its payroll was typically around $18,000 a month. The oldest gold mine was in Blewett, and in 1908, its yield

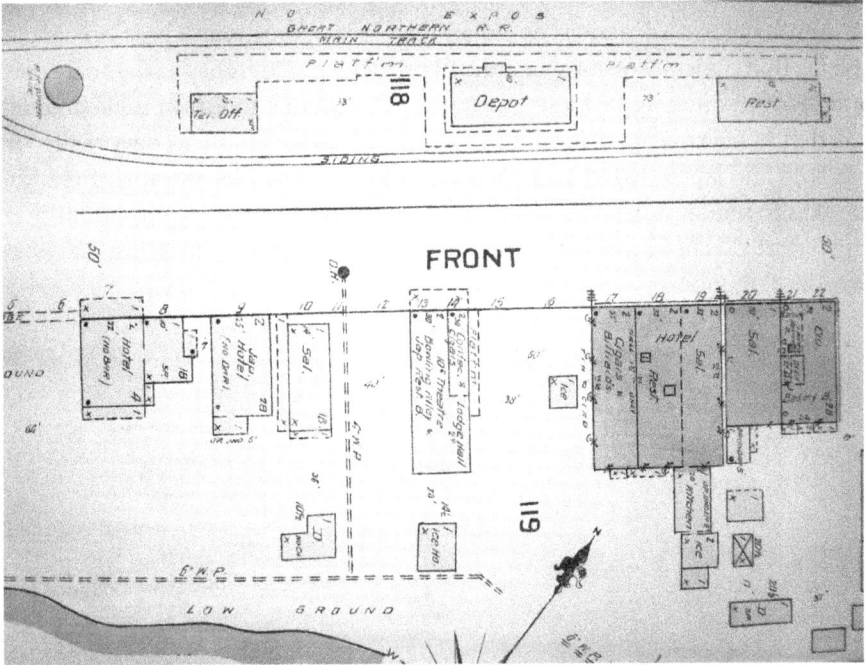

This hard-to-find Sanborn Insurance map shows early Leavenworth in 1909. *From left to right*: hotel, Japanese hotel, saloon, theater, bowling alley, Japanese restaurant, lodge hall, confections and cigars, cigars and billiards, hotel, saloon and restaurant, saloon, barbershop with an oven and bakery in the back. Near the tracks are the Great Northern Railroad Telegraph Office buildings, as well as the depot and restaurant. *Courtesy of Library of Congress.*

in gold had already totaled a whopping $1.5 million. Ambitious farmers had already planted over 165,000 fruit trees in the small radius of just four square miles and had plans to plant more. One of the first white settlers in Wenatchee, Philip Miller, planted numerous apple trees there in 1872. Currently, Washington State grows 125 million boxes of apples per year. At 40 pounds per box, it comes to 2.5 million tons of apples per year. Miller had no idea he had started something that would become so big.

Ghost stories, urban legends and folklore exist in any town, big or small, new or old—human beings are fascinated with the afterlife and are eager to capture proof of the spirit world. Apparitions or odors are the most common forms of paranormal activity. When an animal or a person keeps reappearing at a location over and over again, it is classified as an actual haunting.

An important characteristic of a classic haunting is noises. These noises imitate the sounds of human, environmental and animal activities such as crying, chairs moving, dishes breaking and even barking.

Another form of activity is called the crisis apparition. These are single events that typically occur when the living person undergoes a personal crisis and a loved one's apparition appears to offer them comfort in their time of need. These crisis apparitions are commonly shrugged off as daydreams or ignored and labeled as strange flukes caused by stress. The amount of energy it takes to manifest from the other side is extreme, so it is very important that any effort executed from the spirit be acknowledged and the ghost be given words of thanks.

PART I
THE GHOSTS OF
LEAVENWORTH'S PAST

G hosts in this town consist of the many hardworking and visionary pioneers who left their mark on the town from the late 1800s up through today. In the 1890s, the population of Icicle was around two hundred. Some of the original pioneers were Doctor Hoxsey, George Briskey, J.E. Schubert, Frank Losekamp, Nick Kinscherf, Charles Freytag, John Emig, Ezra Brusha, George Persinger and, of course, Captain Leavenworth. The

Leavenworth in its very early stages around 1906. The two-story brick building on the corner housed the Tumwater Bank, the Chikamin Hotel, a grocery store and the L.D. Company Store built by pioneer Loskamp. Down the street is Moore Company, Elliot and, at the end, a store boasting "Suits made to order!" *Courtesy of Leavenworth Chamber of Commerce.*

Early photograph of Main Street of downtown Leavenworth. In 1892, Captain Leavenworth bought a forty-acre tract that soon became the business district. He then went into mining in Idaho. J.D. Wheeler photo. *Courtesy of Skykomish Historical Society.*

original townwas situated near the junction of the Icicle and Wenatchee Rivers (about one mile south of current-day Leavenworth).

In 1892, two Spokane real estate men named Samuel T. Arthur and Alonzo Murphy purchased the town. Fearing they had made a hasty purchase, they quickly sold it to a man from Portland, Oregon, named Charles Leavenworth. Captain Leavenworth bought the forty-acre parcel that was to soon become the area's business district, strategically placed across from the tracks of the Great Northern Railroad. He wanted to make sure his name lived on. And it certainly has.

1
TUMWATER INN RESTAURANT

I feel that our bodies are a vehicle that holds our soul.
—*Sandy Owens-Carmody, Tumwater Inn owner*

Classified as Leavenworth's oldest restaurant, for over one hundred years the building has been a favorite eatery and hangout for many people. Located now at 219 Ninth Street on the corner of Commercial in downtown Leavenworth, the current owner, Sandy Owens-Carmody, has successfully run the Tumwater for almost thirty years. Many local rumors over the years from old-timers, employees and patrons consist of tales of a spirit who likes to play the piano and move glassware and objects around the bar and kitchen areas.

GHOST STORIES FROM THE CURRENT OWNER, SANDY

We have two ghosts that hang around here regularly, a man and his wife. I think they are from the 1940s or '50s. There used to be a [possibly the Yes Sir Chevrolet Garage now the Obertal Mall] *car dealership across the street and while her husband worked, his wife would come here and eat lunch and wait for him every day. Locals said they were the closest couple, so much in love. After he passed away, she continued to eat lunch here every day. I think their spirits still connect here because it was such a big part of their lives. At times I can smell perfume when no one else is here.*

Many tales of ghosts linger at this Leavenworth icon. The Tumwater Inn at 219 Ninth Street is one of the oldest bars in town, and old-timers have many a ghostly tale or two about this place. *Author photo.*

An Old Poem

Old perfumes wander back from fields of clover
Seen in the light of suns that long have set;
Beloved ones, whose earthly toil is over,
Draw near, as if they lived among us yet.
Old voices call me, through the dusk returning,
I hear the echoes of departed feet...
—Sarah Doudney, "Between the Lights," circa 1875

Another spirit we have at the Tumwater is also a friendly one. We have an old piano in the lobby built in 1871 by the NW Piano Company. For more than thirty years, during all hours of the day, that piano tends to play a soft tune when no one is at it. It could be just a lovely soul wanting to entertain guests or possibly one of the former piano players in one of the bands that used to play dance music for patrons.

One of my favorite ghost stories is the time I was here alone and was straightening up stock in the back—ketchup, mustard, napkins and things like that. I went out front to do some other things, and when I came back to the store room, all of the condiments were undone and changed round.

Are the friendly spirits of the Tumwater Inn just playing games with Sandy, or would they prefer to have the condiments shelved a different way?

Originally called the Overland Café, it opened in 1911, and the proprietor was a man named John Tabuchi. That September, Harry Osborne took over and changed the name from the Overland Café to the Osborne Café. The café had been closed since the death of the former owner in early September 1911. Osborne teamed up with local proprietor J.B. Violette, and they had great plans to install a new glass storefront and remodel the dining room to "make it the most inviting and attractive dining room in Central Washington," Osborne told a *Leavenworth Echo* reporter on September 29. The men sent out several hundred invitations when they opened to the public on October 15 later that same year.

Harry was particularly fond of offering ladies' tea parties on Saturdays from 3:00 p.m. to 5:00 p.m.—all ladies were welcome. At times, over one hundred elegantly dressed women would participate, and Harry treated them like royalty. This made him a very popular and well-liked man indeed.

When the moon came out, the McDaniel's String Orchestra entertained guests with lively music in the evenings so patrons could dance well into the night.

By November of that year, the Osborne Café was advertising in the *Leavenworth Echo*, "For the best .25 cent meal & the best service & the best coffee you will have to eat at the Osborne Café! Sunday dinners are .50 cents."

Osborne and Violette did so well they soon brought in an authentic French chef from Seattle named Adolphe, who soon delighted the locals with his very fancy cuisine.

In October 1912, J.B. Violette leased the Overland Café to an experienced restaurant lady named Mrs. E. Crawford, who was then conducting the St. Francis Hotel.

Around 1913, the Overland Café was operated by A. Manne, who left the following year to buy a hotel in San Francisco called the Terminal Hotel for $75,000. Unfortunately, while in San Francisco, Manne wrote and then borrowed money on a bum check for $5,000—quickly making enemies in the Bay Area with his scheme. He disappeared from town before authorities could charge him with the crime. It was later revealed that Manne had written a few bad checks in Leavenworth prior to leaving town.

In 1922, a lady named Emma Anderson opened it as the Tumwater Gateway Café. It also had live music and dancing on weekends.

Around the 1940s, the name Tumwater Inn stuck, and the place delighted patrons with a fireside room and dancing now under the glimmer of elegant crystal chandeliers.

Today, the Tumwater Inn is still a very inviting place with a great bar, live music, storytelling and wonderful food—no wonder patrons from its past never want to leave. Stop by and enjoy some of the incredible selection of spirits—of the liquid kind.

If you are lucky, the spirit of one of the musicians from the old McDaniel's String Orchestra will play you a favorite tune on the piano or maybe Chef Adolphe's ghost will move something on your table to entertain you.

2

THE EDELWEISS HOTEL

One of the more well-known and historic haunts is the Edelweiss Hotel, located at 843 Front Street. The building was erected in the early 1900s by Frank Losekamp and has been many different businesses over the years. Formerly a hotel, it has more recently housed a wine store, shops, restaurants and offices. Pioneer Frank Losekamp came to the small town called Icicle in 1891. He was the first to open a general store and also tackled the grueling task of bringing supplies in from Ellensburg on pack mules. He built the first log cabin, which was a mere ten feet by ten feet. Later, he took the role of postmaster, organizing the never-ending mail that came in twice a week by stagecoach. In December 1904, he posted an ad in the *Leavenworth Echo*:

> *The Pioneer Losekamp—I have done business with the people in this vicinity for 15 years. Since I have been here, merchants have come and gone, others will come and go. My business is like the house that was built upon a rock, time nor adversity cannot shake it. I want your business and promise fair treatment and goods at a reasonable price. Yours for future business, F.A. Losekamp.*

At that time, the town had a single muddy street with a few small wooden buildings on either side. The town was then basically located where the 1903 Lamb-Davis Lumber Company & Box Factory once stood (currently Leavenworth's Waterfront Park, which runs along the edge of the Wenatchee River).

Left: Early pioneer Frank Loskamp came to the town of Icicle (Leavenworth's former name) around 1891 and built its first log cabin. Later, he built the prominent Loskamp Building, which housed the Tumwater bank and store. *Courtesy of the* Leavenworth Echo, *October 24, 1919.*

Below: Hotel Edelweiss used to be called the Chikamin Hotel. It was one of the first six buildings to adopt the Bavarian theme. *Courtesy of Leavenworth Chamber of Commerce.*

In the summer of 1906, Losekamp had tons of bricks hauled into town in order to build his new two-story Losekamp Building (located at present-day 843 Front Street). The building housed the Tumwater Bank, L.D. Company Store and a general grocery store.

He was extremely well liked in town but eventually developed other interests, so he also began successfully mining in Elk River, Idaho. Mining became one of his passions, although he continued to support and enjoy Leavenworth for the rest of his life.

As for its past, the building has been known to house the spirits of people that appear to be wearing clothing from the Victorian era, including fancy dresses and hats. When it was a hotel, guests and employees would sometimes hear the hushed sounds of arguing behind closed doors—even though no one was checked into those rooms. In the downstairs areas, people claim to see both a man and women at times—both wearing the same old style of clothing—as well as the eerie feeling of being watched. Are the former building's owners keeping a keen eye on the new owners and making sure everything is up to par?

The location could house many possible spirits of people who loved the building and refuse to leave the humble surroundings, as its history is rich with

Front Street in the old Chikamin Hotel building. There are claims of the ghost of an infant and a man named George. It was supposedly once a brothel and a bank with several shootings. It has been investigated by several paranormal groups. *Author photo.*

multiple operators and countless guests. Rumors of hangings and shootings surround the building as well, and the building has even undergone a few ghost hunting sessions.

In 1906, Losekamp entered into a five-year lease with Ed Westbrook and his wife (from Alaska) for the upper portion of the "Charlotte Block" building. Mr. Westbrook noted to the *Leavenworth Echo* in December 1906 that "the hotel will require $70 to furnish each room, and as there are nearly 30 bedrooms, it will require about $2,500 to run a first-class house and cater to none but the best of trade." A year later, the Westbrooks ambitiously opened their Hotel Franklin at the beginning of 1907.

3

HOTEL FRANKLIN

J ust as advertised, the Hotel Franklin offered well-lit and well-furnished rooms equipped with modern steam heat. A local named Professor Rothen made patrons' stays even more pleasurable by presenting dance lessons to the guests. Mrs. Westbrook soon became successful, and Losekamp felt lucky to have secured such a wonderful tenant for his building.

But the hotel soon took backseat to their business in Alaska, so the Westbrooks sold their interest to a new proprietor named Ira Farmer in June 1907.

Later, in 1909, the Hotel Franklin changed its name to the Chikamin Hotel, and the new proprietor was U.H. Leltwich. The advertisements he ran in the *Leavenworth Echo* in May 1909 boasted "Steam Heat, Electric Lights, Baths and 9 foot long bed sheets!" Apparently the long sheets were a luxury and big hit with patrons.

A man named J.L. Campbell managed the hotel from 1910 until fall 1911, and then a Mrs. Augusta Bryant became the newest proprietor. In early 1912, it changed hands again, and a man named D.C. Town became the operator of the Chikamin Hotel.

In the fall of 1912, the Chikamin Hotel changed hands yet once again. A man named D.S. More from Long Beach, California, closed a deal to become the new proprietor. He stated to the *Leavenworth Echo*, "Since leaving California I have traveled all over the United States looking for a location and Leavenworth looks better to me than any other place I have visited in my travels!" He quickly moved there with his wife and daughter.

The Franklin
"A Homelike Hotel"
Cool, Airy, Outside Rooms
Make our house your house
when in Leavenworth. You'll
like the place.
Very Reasonable Rates
J. B. Violette, Prop.

In 1916, the Franklin Hotel would offer free doctor visit to locals by "bloodless surgeons," who claimed they could cure deafness in sixty days and remedy all sorts of maladies. Wives were required to bring their husbands to any visits. *Courtesy of the* Leavenworth Echo.

Early in 1915, Losekamp reclaimed the hotel and switched back to the former name of Hotel Franklin. Losekamp got busy and spent the next few months overhauling the place. Sparing no expense, he painted, wallpapered and bought all new furniture, beds and linens. He built a new office at the head of the stairs, as well as a reading and lounge room for the pleasure of the ladies. Of the twenty-seven rooms to rent, fourteen had hot and cold water and were located on the street side of the hotel. The Hotel Franklin was scheduled to reopen the second week of December in 1915.

Losekamp spent $4,000 on the remodel, and this included a very fine $300 phonograph. He quaintly woke his guests each morning with the lovely sound of soft music. Later, before he made his way back to Idaho to work his Jericho Mine, he had a state-of-the-art electric sign hung out front so patrons could easily see the hotel from far away. No matter where his business or travels took him, Losekamp always considered Leavenworth, also known as Icicle, his forever home.

In 1917, the adventurous J.B. Violette took over the Hotel Franklin and changed the name to just the Franklin. He boasted that the Franklin was a "homelike hotel with very reasonable rates." In May 1918, a man named J.B. Huff was scheduled to take over managing the Franklin with the assistance of Violette's wife's sister. The building went through many other owners throughout the years. In the late '60s, the building was once again renamed the Chikamin Hotel when LaVerne Peterson bought it. Since the building was in slight despair anyway, she jumped on board with the town's new vision of becoming a German village. For LaVerne, there was no time better than the present to partake in the theme. She soon began approving designs for the remodel.

After the remodel was complete, it was renamed the Hotel Edelweiss and became one of the first Bavarian-themed buildings to make the switch in Leavenworth. The Edelweiss building has recently been sold and will undergo another transformation into a restaurant.

One has to wonder if the mischievous and overly interested spirits that still roam the building are one (or two) of the many people who fell in love with the building and tried hard to make it productive and successful. Is Frank Losekamp still wandering his building making sure the place is clean and tidy and that the new proprietors are treating its patrons with all the newest and finest amenities?

4

LOCAL HOT SPOTS AND OLD HAUNTS IN TOWN

History is full of people who haunt us, who want to be recognized and never forgotten for what they did, what they created, what they offered.

Like most towns in the late 1800s and early 1900s, disputes were often settled by gunpowder. Early pioneer P.M. Soloman started conducting business in the small town of Icicle around 1891. One interesting quote from Soloman about early Leavenworth is from an article posted in the *Leavenworth Echo* on October 24, 1913. His thoughts in 1913 were, "I had a store at the old town Icicle known as the Minnesota Mercantile Co. in 1895. In those days it was certainly a wild and wooly town. Nearly every night there was shooting....[T]he men eventually settled their disagreements with gunpowder."

It is hard to imagine such a welcoming, festive and fun town ever being like that described, but things were certainly handled differently back then. This true of most early towns.

A ghost story from a local: "I was in the elevator very early in the morning and no one else was really around yet. As I was leaving the elevator I heard 'Hello?' There was nobody there to greet me or that could have said this." Perhaps a friendly spirit who was watching their wares? It is said objects can manifest the spirits of the individuals who loved them. When dealing with antiques, it is fascinating to wonder who owned the piece before you and what stories could it tell if it could talk!

THE OPERA HOUSE BAR

The Opera House Bar opened in 1904 and was located on the second lot east of the Losekamp Building on Front Street. Tholin & Smith spent $3,000 on fixtures, real cherry furniture and a beautiful gold leaf sign to make the place as grand as possible. It yearned to have the most luxurious drinking establishment in the whole town.

A few years later in the bar (now renamed just the Opera Bar), on a hot summer night in June 1907, a very intoxicated man named Davis burst into the saloon, and after a few obnoxious words, he shot an innocent bystander named John McGee with a .38-caliber pistol. Eyewitnesses claimed (the ones who bravely hung around) that Davis came up to McGee and started slapping him for another man who was mad at McGee. The confused McGee asked the man to quit slapping him, to no avail. Davis then took off his coat and charged toward McGee. A spectator noticed Davis had a gun, and this is when many patrons ran out of the bar to the safety of the streets. Davis then took his revolver and struck McGee over the head twice. Without further hesitation, Davis shot McGee.

A brave railroad detective tried to grab the gun from Davis, but the attacker was too aggressive and pointed his gun at the detectives face, firing twice. The gun was luckily empty, saving the detective's life. The drunken

"It's the Water"

That Makes

The Opera Bar

The Opera Bar run by Tholin & Smith announced its grand opening on December 3, 1904, and had real cherry furnishings and later a fancy gold lead sign. In 1907, it was the place of the murder of John McGee. An intoxicated man named Davis mistook him for someone else and shot him in cold blood. *Courtesy of the Leavenworth Echo.*

Davis was promptly arrested by Deputy Sheriff W.O. Platt. The injured McGee was quickly taken to the overworked Doctor Hoxsey's office to be examined and treated for the wound. Davis was taken from Leavenworth to Cashmere, then on to Wenatchee by freight train with Deputy Dubois at his side. The judge was awakened and the assailant charged.

In the morning, when locals heard of the attack, many prayed that the well-liked and hardworking McGee would survive his mysterious assault. Unfortunately, the fifty-four-year-old carpenter died. He had just moved to Leavenworth the year prior from Seattle. Davis had also recently moved to Leavenworth from Kentucky, but he was known to have caused trouble before. Rumors had circulated that Davis had been on a two-week drinking binge prior to the murder.

The *Leavenworth Echo* disclosed on December 26, 1913, that "Former Leavenworth Man Pardoned…Governor Lister signed a conditional pardon of W.L. Davis who shot and killed John McGee."

McGee was reported to be a quiet, small man, while Davis was over six feet tall. Davis's family stated in the same *Echo*, "He is guiltless of murderous intent." The court trial lasted several days, and many tears were shed by Davis's family. Davis was encouraged to plead insanity. Jurors sat speechless. Prosecuting Attorney Crass was at Davis's side as he and his sister cried together. There was some sympathy for the prisoner by locals. When his wife appeared, she ran to Davis and threw her arms around him, creating a dramatic scene.

But the good Judge Steiner, new to the case, was not so easily swayed by these tactics. The *Wenatchee Daily World* reported the judge's comments: "I do not see how the jury could find that you were so insane at the time that you are not to be responsible for your actions…where insanity is of such a slight nature that it doesn't amount to much. It is NO excuse for the concession of a crime! The lawyers wasted two days to make something out of nothing."

On August 30, 1907, the *Echo* reported, "Davis decided to plead guilty of murder in the second degree. He was given a sentence of 20 years hard labor in the Walla Walla State Penitentiary." A few weeks later, thirty-year-old Davis began having heart trouble, and the doctor doubted he would recover. Davis stated he didn't mean to do it and would "rather take McGee's place than where he is."

Years after the murder, in 1911, the new owner, J.W. Elliot, had grand plans on replacing the wood building with brick and was going to improve it. He spent $15,000 realizing his dream.

It is interesting to take note that in 1905 a new sheriff named Webb was appointed along with his Deputy Teshera. The Commissioner's Court appointed these men $30 per month toward their salaries. In 1911, the cost of running the sheriff's department for the year was a mere $5,575.40.

The Scenic Theatre

In the early 1900s, the Scenic Theatre started entertaining locals with its lively performances. In 1909, M.B. Hake ordered a Victrola that the group used in the singing performances. In 1911, one of the theater's best hits was *All a Mistake*, performed by the Leavenworth Amateur Dramatic Club. Later, management announced that the theater would run six thousand feet of film each night for twenty-five cents. A few years later, theater manager and

The Scenic Theatre

The grand entrance to the Scenic Theatre with manager W.B. Simpson in the foreground. It seems the Scenic began operation around 1909. In 1910, it boasted the purchase of the finest Victrola to accompany the singers. It was packed every night by locals and tourists. Many famous talents entertained on the stage. *Courtesy of the* Leavenworth Echo.

performing actor Mr. Simpson added a beautiful drop curtain and ordered a $1,000 Chickering grand piano. (Could this be the same Chickering piano that now resides at the Tumwater Inn?) Mr. Simpson was routinely heard saying that "Nothing is too good for the Scenic Theatre or Leavenworth!" and locals packed the seats every night. The *Echo* announced on October 18, 1912, "Vaudeville performances, motion pictures shows, pictures of the Gans-Nelson fight, entertainment by the 'human ostrich' and the famous play 'The Awakening of Helena Richie' with actors Roselle Knott and Henry Hall would be available with ticket prices being $1 on the lower floor and .75 cents for balcony seats."

It would not be surprising (knowing how actors and actresses can never get enough of the stage) if some of these entertainers still roam the streets of their beloved town a century later, begging for some recognition and maybe even applause.

OLD BARCLAY HOTEL

The beautiful brick building at 833 Front Street that houses Simply Found, a wonderful boutique, was once the Barclay Hotel, which boasted a theater and pool hall.

In 1913, Mr. Barclay started building the three-story brick building (adjacent to the Leavenworth Meat Market at that time) and proudly installed the first elevator in town. The top floor was to be thirty-three hotel rooms, and the main floor was divided into two sections: a lobby and sample room and a moving picture show room. In the basement, he planned on creating a bowling alley and barbershop. Although Barclay conducted work in Seattle, he still invested much time, energy and money in his properties in Leavenworth. By 1914, it would house a full basement and the thirty-three daylight rooms upstairs that would have electric lighting, steam heat and both hot and cold running water.

A.C. Barclay, one of Leavenworth's most ambitious men, was not only proprietor of the hotel but also ran a movie theater and an auto service and was director of the Amalgamated Gold Mine. He was known years later as one of the oldest Great Northern Railroad conductors and knew everybody in town, man, woman or child. He left Leavenworth for ten years but later returned to his favorite place to resume business.

Hotel Barclay

A. C. BARCLAY, Prop.

The Barclay Hotel, 1919, was located at 833 Front Street and boasted that all thirty-three rooms had hot and cold running water. Rates in 1914 for transients were fifty cents per day. *Courtesy of the Leavenworth Echo.*

In 1915, the building suffered a small fire in the basement, but no one was harmed. A Dr. Edward de Reymonte took a room in the fall of 1917 to deliver his wonderful healing talents. He advertised himself in the *Echo* on September 11, 1914, as a "Drugless Physician and Bloodless Surgeon."

In April 1920, Barclay felt the need to house more patrons, so he decided to build an addition to the hotel. This would provide the space to accommodate another one hundred guests with its fifty rooms. The new building opened in the fall of the same year.

When the Bavarian theme transformation hit Leavenworth, the building was a PUD (Public Utility District) building owned by the Herretts and then became the beautiful Europa Hotel.

The brick Barclay Building still thrives and is just as lovely today as the day it was built.

It is said that people have felt very cold chills and the building houses a friendly but mischievous spirit. Could this be the hardworking Mr. Barclay making sure the patrons are well taken care of?

5

THE ONE-HUNDRED-PLUS-YEAR-OLD UNSOLVED MURDER OF CHAS GORDON, LEAVENWORTH PROPRIETOR

On the bitter cold night of Wednesday, December 9, 1914, the sounds of a fatal gunshot rang through the halls of the Overland Hotel at 7:30 p.m. in Leavenworth and Chas. L. Gordon, proprietor of the Leavenworth Bar, was murdered in cold blood.

The century-old unsolved murder was witnessed by twenty-one people, none of whom saw the violent perpetrator in action or witnessed him fleeing from the scene of the crime. How can there be twenty-one people nearby (as well as other people in the street) and no one saw anything? Maybe they knew who it was and were just too afraid to speak up.

Gordon lay quietly on the ground as he waited the long thirty minutes for the arrival of the doctor. Charlie had only been a resident of Leavenworth for about one year and was well respected and liked by all who knew him. So what exactly happened? And why?

Just minutes prior to his murder, Mr. and Mrs. Gordon and three of their friends were eating a nice meal and talking quietly together at a table. One of them, Dora Armstrong, suddenly felt a very cold draft, so she got up to find out where the chilly air was coming from. She quickly found a door that was open to the street outside. When she went to close the door, someone on the inside warned her, "Do not shut that door." Startled, she quickly returned to their table and told the others what had happened.

Mr. Gordon bravely went to see what the problem was and to see about closing the door to make things more comfortable for the ladies. Just seconds later, Gordon was shot in the chest at close range by a twelve-gauge shotgun and left to die in the hallway. The sound of unexpected gunshot made everyone freeze in their seats.

When Gordon did not return to their table, the group panicked. Irene, unfazed that she could be next to be killed, ran to the hallway only to find her poor husband bleeding profusely. Hearing the shot, one of the first people to arrive at the crime scene was William O'Rourke, proprietor of the nearby Rainier Café in town. As reported in the *Leavenworth Echo* on December 11, 1914, "Gordon's wife Irene testified that while she lay at his side and asked, 'Charlie, who shot you?' His reply? 'I don't know, but I bet a million dollars Richards' done this!'"

Soon Doctor Hoxsey was at Charlie's side to administer aid, but he professionally concluded that the wound was surely fatal, so the smart doctor focused on trying to get information about Gordon's murderer from him before his untimely death. Gordon's final words were "I am dying... and the person who shot me fired from that room!" He pointed to room down the hall and continued to chant "Richards! Richards! Richards the plumber shot me!"

Gordon was pointing in the direction of room 21. Who rented room 21 on 4:00 p.m. that fatal Wednesday? Locals stated that the unknown occupant was short, dark and heavyset and sported a short moustache.

It took about fifteen more minutes for the busy Sheriff Bohnsack to arrive. Although the gun was left on the floor in room 21, the true ownership of the double-barrel shotgun was never discovered. Upon further inspection of the gun, Bohnsack discovered that it still had one shell left in it. There was also a long rope tied to the bedpost that was left hanging from an open window down to the street below. When the street was inspected, there were no fresh footprints in the snow and no sign of the rope being used, as it was still covered with a light coating of frost.

Obviously, the murderer had escaped another way. Who was this mysterious man who rented room 21? Why were there over twenty witnesses but not enough information to develop even one suspect? Later, when Richards the plumber was questioned, he firmly stated that he was home by about 5:00 p.m. that day and never returned to Leavenworth.

When Gordon arrived at Leavenworth, he eagerly bought the Leavenworth Bar. He had only owned it one year before his death. After Gordon's murder, the bar was sold back to its former owner S.E. Ritchie, just days after Gordon's death. Although Gordon's wife remained the owner of the building, Ritchie wasted no time buying back the bar's stock and all of its fixtures. The plot thickens.

Would his desire for the return of the Leavenworth Bar be a motive for Ritchie to murder Charlie or simply pure coincidence? Was Gordon just in the wrong place at the wrong time? If so, what was the killer doing with the shotgun? If Gordon was not the killer's actual target, then who was? And who was the mysterious person who whispered to the nervous Miss Armstrong not to close the door? The killer himself or an accomplice?

We will never know.

Many public letters written to Mrs. Gordon after his death present Mr. Gordon as kind, generous, personable and friendly. The unsolved murder is truly a sad story and one case that will never be closed. Charlie was from Upstate New York and moved to Leavenworth in March 1914. He purchased the Leavenworth Bar from Ritchie & Churchill soon after his arrival.

Just a few months before Charlie's murder, Irene Gordon purchased the summer resort called Lake Wenatchee Club House in August 1914—a beautiful property on twenty-three acres—for just $6,500. She planned on improving the resort by adding two tennis courts. Mr. Gordon is buried at the North Road Cemetery in Leavenworth.

6

THE OVERLAND HOTEL AND BAR

The building holding the Overland Bar carries quite the history of various proprietors, businesses, patrons, multiple fires and rebuilds and even a few deaths—so many details that it is hard to cover and keep track of.

In 1904, the building caught fire, and the owner, Bjork, suffered a loss of $3,500 plus another $1,500 in fixtures. He had no insurance at the time. That fall, a Mr. Fritz was running the bar and had just invested in new solid oak furnishings and fixtures. It boasted to be "one of the best hotels between Seattle and Spokane." It offered thirty-one rooms on the upper floor, and downstairs had a large kitchen, office and dining room. Since the recent fire in town, Leavenworth had been without a hotel to cater to eager patrons.

An adventurous team decided to open the Leavenworth Café in February 1906 in the smaller section of the building adjacent to the hotel. This was the store room formerly occupied by Plisch & Bliss. The name Overland Café was attached to several different locations over the years.

In December 1906, another fire broke out in the building next to the Overland Hotel in a restaurant operated by McCabe & Company. Charles and Plisch were the owners of the building at this time. To attest to the superior advantage of building with brick over wood, the nearby building suffered a complete loss, while the Overland only suffered fifty dollars in damage.

In the summer of 1907, the Overland changed hands again, and Bjork sold to Walker (from Seattle) and Barthel (a local railroad worker).

Overland Hotel
Mrs. Irene Gordon, Prop.
Modern in Every Respect
Steam Heat—Hot and cold running water in each room.

Special Rates
41 comfortable rooms
$8, $10 and $12 per mo.
Leavenworth's Leading Hotel. Opposite the Depot.

The Overland Bar & Hotel was opposite the railroad depot and the site of the unsolved 1914 murder of a well-loved business owner named C.L. Gordon. J.B. Violette was the proprietor and boasted the largest selection of alcohol and forty-two rooms at twelve dollars per month. *Courtesy of the* Leavenworth Echo, *October 23, 1914.*

In a *Leavenworth Echo* from March 1907, Fritz, the new owner, placed an ad that read, "Always keep a bottle of I.W. Harper Whiskey in sight. Good to look at and good to taste; and what's more, it's a benefit to your health. Sold by J.G. Fritz at Overland Bar." Fritz later closed a deal with a new interested party, J.B. Violette, who was a former sheriff from North Bend and proprietor for the Overland Hotel and Bar.

Harry Osbourne soon went into business with J.B. Violette for the Overland right after the most recent owner passed away, and they switched its name to the Osborne. They remodeled the café with a new glass front and new carpets.

The fatal fire at the Overland in December 1913 (which killed a Blewett prospector named Johnston and a few others) caused another $10,000 loss on the building for Mr. Bjork and $1,000 loss for J.B. Violette, who ran the Overland Bar at the time.

The hotel saw other action, too. In April 1913, the *Leavenworth Echo* reported, "At 5 pm Monday afternoon a man named Kline (who was the General Manager of Lamb-Davis Lumber Co at the time) walked into the Tumwater Bank with a .38 caliber pistol in hand. Soon a man named Riggs walked in. Kline threatened to shoot Riggs if he didn't leave." Unsurprisingly, Kline shot him. Luckily, the bullet only went through his shoulder, and the forty-seven-year-old Riggs made his way back to the Overland Hotel, where he awaited the doctor.

In 1914, another fire broke out, causing damage to many buildings. Irene Gordon (the wife of the murdered Charlie Gordon) was the operator of the Overland Hotel at the time. The building was directly opposite the train depot in town. It offered forty-one rooms with hot and cold water and steam heat. It was the largest and most up-to-date hotel in town.

J.B. Violette operated the bar for some time, partaking in the occasional violation when the town went through its dry period. Violette was a prominent businessman in Leavenworth for many years. He often posted quirky ads in the newspaper extolling the greatness of whiskey. In 1916, Violette was raided at his home and the police confiscated thirty-two bottles of beer, seventy-five bottles of whiskey, card tables and poker chips.

Proprietor J.B. Violette was very active in the community and managed many hotels and bars. He moved to Leavenworth in 1908 and bought a home as well as a ten-acre apple orchard one mile south of town. *Courtesy of the* Leavenworth Echo.

7
THE HAUNTED CEMETERIES

There are two Leavenworth Cemeteries. One is known as the North Road Cemetery, and the other is Pioneer Cemetery, which has also been called Tumwater Cemetery and Mission Cemetery. (Please be respectful and do not disturb any graves, go ghost hunting or trespass on these properties.)

LEAVENWORTH CEMETERY

In the late 1800s, the Leavenworth Cemetery became the final resting place to numerous unfortunate railroad workers. People have told stories of eerie phantom lights, similar to the old-time lanterns the workers used to carry. Others tell of hearing the faint hammering of railroad spikes in tune with the whistling that often came from workers while they were building the railroad.

The following is a ghost story retold from an article written by William Chandler in the *Leavenworth Echo* on June 16, 1916, titled "A Phantom Train?":

A little farmer boy named John Philips was fishing in a small boat by the old collapsed railroad bridge outside of town. The bridge had suffered some years before and the unfortunate engine and 2 cars went plunging into the icy river below. Although the bridge was partially rebuilt, it was never used again. Young John heard a distance choo choo, and knowing the bridge was

The Leavenworth Cemetery during a beautiful day. Some claim to see eerie lanterns late at night. *Author photo.*

unusable, panicked. He saw the train, clouds of steam swirling into the air, coming from behind a clump of trees.

The train moved forward over the bridge then quickly crashed over the side and into the river. John had heard many rumors of the phantom train. Although it was hard to believe, he realized this must be the ghost train!

Suddenly he spotted a small girl who was soaked in water. She was not scared by all this commotion. When John asked the girl about the crash she laughed. He said, "Great Scott! How can you laugh at such a terrible thing!" She quietly responded, "I am the spirit of one who years ago went down with the train that crashed into the river from that bridge."

John, in shock, dropped his oars.

"Take up your oars. Carry me to yonder bank that from there I may go back to my resting place in the cemetery."

Apparently the girl was the one who had been carried down the stream to her death. John, shocked, recognized her image from a photograph he had seen earlier.

The Leavenworth North Road Cemetery

Many pioneers and railroad workers are buried in the town they loved. Some say they can hear the faint sounds of workers whistling and see a hint of a lantern's light swaying in the chill of the night. Are these possibly the lost souls of workers still clocking in to work on the tracks? Stroll through the grounds and search for some of the names in this book and pay your respects for all their hard work, time and energy produced to create such a glorious town for all to enjoy.

Hardworking railway unidentified crew members pose in front of Locomotive 563 in Stevens County. *Courtesy of Washington State Digital Archives, Locomotive 563, 1900–1930, State Library Photograph Collection, Crossroads on the Columbia, item # scpa00800001004.*

Lifelong Friendship to the End

A wonderful story about best friends is the lifelong but tragic friendship of John Johnston and John Heavner. Johnston and Heavner were residents and mining partners of Blewett for more than twenty years. They were lucky and did extremely well in the gold business and owned valuable property together. As a teenager, Johnston had originally come to Blewett from Sweden.

In 1913, they uncovered many nuggets—ranging anywhere from fifty cents to seven dollars in value—and that was only the beginning. The men continued mining together and lived peacefully in Blewett. Both men were kind and never caused any disagreements in town. Their mine supplied enough gold that the two men never had to worry about money troubles. It was possibly not the smartest thing to do, but on more than one occasion, Johnston would secretly show people his buckskin poke full of gold nuggets.

They were inseparable for over twenty years, but Johnston lost his life in a tragic fire to smoke inhalation at the Overland Hotel in 1914. He had come to town that week to replenish his camp and mining supplies. Since the miner was tired, he decided to stay the night at the Overland and head out in the early morning instead. He took room 15 and bunked down for the evening.

That cold Tuesday evening on the last day of December 1914, the Overland Hotel caught fire. As the fire raged, another man staying at the hotel, Jack Heaton, tried in vain to wake poor Johnston but finally gave up, as the room was quickly filling with smoke. Jack ran downstairs to safety. Johnston's body was found Thursday morning. One or two other miners perished in the blaze, their names unknown. The building was owned by Bjork and managed by J.B. Violette at the time. The fire destroyed the hotel and five businesses with a loss of $60,500.

Johnston was buried in the North Road Cemetery in Leavenworth. Heavner, in his deepest sorrow, vowed to be buried next to his partner. Heavner ordered a special tombstone for his comrade and went into town from Blewett to Leavenworth to place the stone. The very sad Heavner also gave instructions that he be buried next to Johnston when his time came to pass into the afterlife. His attempts to drown his sorrows were reported in the *Leavenworth Echo* on May 21, 1915:

> *Heavner devoted his time to bowling and drinking freely. He purchased a bottle of whiskey and headed back to their mining camp in Blewett. As he made his way, he discovered he had accidentally left this bottle at the post office on his way out of town. He tried to retrieve the whiskey on Saturday as Heavner had been drinking quite a lot since his friend's death in order to stop the anguish and pain of his loss. When he was in town he would tell people he "just wants to be with Johnston."*

Some speculated that he tried to drink his way into the afterlife so he could be reunited with his best friend. The next day, poor sixty-eight-year-old Heavner was found dead on the floor of their cabin after falling from his chair. The interesting part of this story is that he accidentally knocked over an oil lamp during his fall, which should have caught the place on fire, leaving Heavner to same horrible demise as his partner.

Did his lifelong friend, Johnston, come back from the grave to protect his friend from also burning to death? How did the flame from the oil lamp magically extinguish itself? Could a drunk person who fell so hard that he died, in the midst of that fall, have enough time and wits about him to extinguish the burning flame of an overturned oil lamp?

It would be wonderful to believe that his friend and partner, even after he passed into another dimension, returned at Heavner's time of need in order to protect him. The men are buried side by side, just as Heavner wished, at the North Road Cemetery. The whereabouts of their gold is a mystery.

The body of Chas. L. Gordon, who was murdered at the Overland Hotel in 1914, is also buried at this cemetery.

OTHER HAUNTED CEMETERIES

Thorp Cemetery

The rumor that is shared around campfires is that the ghostly image of a Native American woman named Suzy can often be seen here. Supposedly, she was hanged in the late 1890s and can now be spotted once again on her white horse. Some say that if they listen carefully late at night they can even hear the muffled cries of her sobbing in despair.

Roslyn Cemetery

This is the final resting place for many unfortunate miners whose lives were lost in mining disasters. The biggest mining disaster in Washington State's history occurred in May 1892 and claimed the lives of 45 miners. Another tragedy in October 1909 claimed the lives of 10 more men, who were buried in the town. At the time, blacks and whites had to be buried in separate cemeteries. It is noted that approximately 50,000 coal miners in the United States risked and gave their lives on the job between the years of 1870 and 1914. That comes to 1,136 men per year who died for the sake of coal to fuel the locomotives. This number does NOT include the number of accidents incurred, just fatalities. It is said over 100,000 accidents burdened the workers in the damp and dangerous mining conditions. The working conditions were very poor back then. Many lives were lost, and the deceased were separated into divisions before their burial.

Roslyn has nineteen acres devoted to the dead and an interesting system for its cemeteries. It boasts twenty-six cemeteries in all, and the bodies are buried in plots determined by different factors including race, fraternal orders and even cultures. When one strolls through these beautiful and eerie cemeteries, the gravestones provide more than the basic information of the buried. Many have intricately carved head stones with poems, photographs, interesting epithets and trinkets left by loved ones.

As you mosey through the beautiful burial ground, take a moment to pause and think of these brave men who worked so hard and how their lives were tragically cut short, leaving many grieving women, children, family members and friends behind. Upon research, many of these men were just teenagers when they lost their lives.

A Ghost Story from Annette D. in Bothell, Washington

I always stop at cemeteries when traveling through towns. I find them beautiful and somewhat peaceful. When I was younger we lived next door from a cemetery, and I would amuse myself on boring days by taking my box of crayons and pieces of paper and wandering the cemetery to make gravestone rubbings. My mother never made fun of me or said they were sad or creepy. She also found many of them beautiful. At night by the fire, she would read the rubbings to me if they had a poem or quote. I loved to rub any angel designs I could find. When I stopped at the Roslyn Cemetery, I did not have any crayons or paper like in my younger days (now I just take my cellphone in the hopes of catching a ghostly apparition!) and as I was walking around I swore I heard a woman crying off to the left, just behind me. At first I thought, "Oh that poor woman. She must have just lost her husband or something." I turned around to see her and maybe smile or nod a gesture her way out of kindness, but no one was there. The only person I could see was a man some was away, certainly not within distance of hearing him. I took a few pictures with my phone but nothing came of them. When I returned to my car, I looked up the history of Roslyn and discovered many tragic mining accidents that killed many men. Almost fifty men lost in the two big explosions. Some of their bodies were never found. I am sure that many are buried right there in that cemetery. I still wonder if those cries were from the ghost of a woman who lost her husband in the explosion and still sits by his grave mourning to this day. So terribly sad.

Location

From eastbound I-90 take the Roslyn/Salmon la Sac exit 80; go left on Bullfrog Road, through the roundabout; and take the second turn off in the second roundabout to Roslyn on WA-903. Continue a mile until Pennsylvania Avenue. Once in town, head west past the Roslyn Museum (better yet, stop at the Roslyn Museum, too, at 203 West Pennsylvania Avenue (509) 649-2355) and proceed up the hill into Fifth Street, taking a left on Memorial Drive.

East Wenatchee Cemetery

Many soldiers are said to be buried in this cemetery. Locals confess to seeing the image of a general-type apparition wandering the graveyard alone. At night, shadows of people dressed in white appear. A man dressed in an army uniform has been seen roaming around the soldiers' graves, possibly grieving over the loss of his men. On the west side, a dark figure has been seen wandering through the nearby orchards.

8

THE HORRIBLE FIRES OF DOWNTOWN LEAVENWORTH

This book would not be complete without acknowledging the town of Leavenworth's remarkable comeback from many devastating fires and losses. It's miraculous how many times the little town suffered substantial loss from fires and continued to rebuild itself over and over again. In the early 1900s, firemen risked their lives with questionable equipment and supplies for a mere $6.50 per day wage. From a city council meeting they created Ordinance No. 132 on February 17, 1914, which mandated a volunteer fire department of not more than twenty-four members to be paid $0.50 per hour while engaging in fighting fires.

During some of the worst fires, the men had to try to fight the flames with hoses that didn't couple properly to the few hydrants in town (as they were often different sizes), forcing the men to struggle with brass reducers. Water at times could be scarce. Sometimes the weather was so cold in Leavenworth that the hoses would accumulate small masses of ice in them, shutting off the flow of water completely, rendering the hoses useless.

The *Leavenworth Echo* reported massive fires over and over again year after year—each time Leavenworth promptly and quickly rebuilt itself. Finally, toward the last of the disasters, it reemerged brick by brick instead of the easy-to-burn wood.

The first fire in Leavenworth occurred in November 1894. A frame building on Big Rock corner destroyed a barbershop and a jewelry store. Both had no insurance. There was no real means of a fire department, so citizens had to watch as the buildings went up in flames, unable to do anything to stop the fires. One story goes that citizens had to throw snowballs at a building that was burning down in order to try to help.

An untimely fire on Thanksgiving Day in 1896 cremated seven buildings, also without insurance. This blaze occurred on the same block as the 1894 fire. The Overland Hotel, Bisbee & Donahoe's Saloon, Posey's Barber Shop, Severton's Saloon, Mrs. Andersons Restaurant and Duffy's Saloon were destroyed. Unfortunately, there were a few tragic deaths, as the firefighters of that era still had little to work with.

One Sunday afternoon in December 1902, more fire tragedy struck the town. Of these buildings destroyed were a restaurant, a millinery owned by Mrs. Beamish, G.C. Merriam, J.W. Poag Confectionary and Doctor Hoxsey's valuable library and much-needed medical instruments.

On another blustery January morning in 1904, at 6:00 a.m., seven more buildings burned, (in the same area that burned in 1896), and the town took another huge loss. The blaze started at Adam's and Burke's Hall. First at the scene were two of Great Northern crew members John Nelson and Jay Wyckoff. It spread to the American Hotel to the west. The Lobby Saloon at the west end of the row owned by Walker suffered, as well as Plisch & Bliss, the Bloom Meat Market and Bjork of the Overland Hotel. Most had no insurance to help with their damages, and the figures were around $25,000 in losses.

Flames burned once again in June in the same year, and it was considered one of the most devastating fires to locals. Starting in the Leavenworth Mercantile's wood warehouse on Front Street, the blaze was discovered by a Seattle drummer named Babb around 1:30 a.m. The fire destroyed some of the brick Mercantile and the City Drug Store (which also housed the Tholin & Smith Saloon and had lodging rooms upstairs—all occupied at the time of the fire). Nelson's Law Office, Greeves Barber Shop, the Tumwater Café, a private residence and the Cascade Hotel located behind these buildings burned to the ground. Pioneer Frank Losekamp suffered severe burns on both of his hands trying to help with the recue efforts.

The city had experienced enough. With no real adequate system in place, the town was destined to always be at mercy of the flames. A meeting was pulled together at a local barbershop to organize a crew and secure a hose and cart. J.B. Adams was appointed the first fire chief, and thirty-four volunteers signed up.

More tragedy struck in late December 1906 at 5:00 p.m. in a building adjacent to the Overland Hotel that was a restaurant occupied by McCabe & Company and owned by Charles Plisch at the time. The thirty-four-foot-tall Bloom & Tuck Building was a two-story located on the west side of the restaurant that had about forty feet of space between it and the fire. With that and the organization of the firemen, they were able to save the Lobby Saloon, the Samantha Saloon and the Clifford House from flames. The managers of the Lobby Saloon were quick in thinking and moved $2,000 worth of liquor out and under a nearby sidewalk for safety. The Leavenworth Café was destroyed by the fire.

In 1907, more requests for equipment went out to councils and boards requesting funding for much-needed proper fire equipment. Learning from their losses, most residents replaced wooden structure with brick ones, and in 1909, several brick buildings cropped up on Front Street.

In the spring of 1912, another fire destroyed two business buildings: Grant's tailor shop (where the fire started) and Mrs. Case's Millinery Store. The nearby Leavenworth Furniture & Hardware Company and J.D. Wheeler's Photo Gallery came very close to becoming char as well.

In the summer of 1914, six more buildings burned. The town and business owners must have felt helpless, as it was the third fire in the same spot. It started in the rear of the rebuilt Lobby Saloon (opposite the train depot) and moved quickly to the Clifford Hotel, the Big Bloom Building and the Overland Hotel (once again). Luckily, the brick addition to the Overland Hotel stopped the flames from spreading. Tumwater Light & Water Company did experience a loss, too, with poles and wires being damaged.

But the town was to endure even more blazes, unfortunately. In the fall of 1914, the Roach's Shoe and Harness Store took to flames about 1:30 a.m., originating in the upstairs hall. Roach's was located between the three-story brick Barclay Hotel (now 833 Front Street) and the two-story brick King Block.

It was a total loss.

Townspeople started to fear they had a firebug on their hands—and for good reason. More fires plagued the town; one at Hub's Clothing Store, then Seeley's Tin Shop and later a fire in the Brown's Livery Barn that also burned Lou Bender's blacksmith shop and one house. This fire tragically also killed two horses.

New Years Day in 1915 was nothing to celebrate for some citizens. Leavenworth locals woke to more terrifying blazes—this time one of the worst. The Bjork Business Block was up in smoke and flames at 3:00 a.m. and completely destroyed. The block consisted of the new Overland Hotel (the largest and oldest hotel in the city during that time), as well as two saloons, a poolroom and a restaurant. John Johnston, a well-liked miner from Blewett, and two local men lost their lives in the fire.

As reported in the *Leavenworth Echo* on January 1, 1915, the losses for the buildings were $33,000 to John Bjork; the Overland Bar owned by J.B. Violette was completely destroyed loss at $10,000; Chas. Nichol owned the Windmill Pool Room with a loss of $4,500; and the Lobby Bar reported a loss of $8,000. Widow Irene Gordon was running the Overland Hotel and took a loss of $5,000. There was also a small Japanese restaurant that burned down. There was inadequate, if any, insurance on some of these buildings. Soon gasses had accumulated, causing a terrible explosion.

By 5:00 p.m., it was all over and done. In just a few hours, with firemen and locals doing everything they could, the Bjork Block Building was gone.

All of these devastating fires took both a financial and emotional toll on the townspeople of Leavenworth, but through determination and hard work, their city was reborn building by building. The spirits of these firefighters, citizens and business owners should always be remembered and respected because it is probably they who still roam the streets and businesses of downtown making sure everything and everyone is safe and sound.

9

LOCAL LEAVENWORTH PIONEERS

The early pioneers of Leavenworth and surrounding areas may or may not be still strolling through their favorite towns, but it would be a shame to not include them. These adventurous men and women believed in the future of their beloved cities and worked hard to promote them.

It is hard to prove or disprove that the spirits that loiter up and down the sidewalks and in and out of the buildings are some of the pioneers that might still making sure everything is in order and running smoothly. Some of the well-known pioneers for Leavenworth were Doctor Hoxsey, George Briskey, J.E. Schubert, Nick Kinscherf, Chas. Freytag, John Emig, Frank Losekamp, Ezra Brusha and George Persinger and, of course, Captain Leavenworth himself.

Other hardworking businessmen who helped Leavenworth in its early stages were shoemaker P.H. Graham; general manager Harry Moore (1906); Adam & Carr Real Estate; G.W. Hathaway, who opened a cigar and tobacco shop nest to the Opera House Bar; and E.N. Burgess, who was a very popular barber. George Keating moved from Everett in 1904 and later opened a hardware store on the corner of Ninth and Front. Keating, being a productive man, installed a new "luxuriant up-to-date porcelain-lined affair with hot and cold connections" bathtub in Gilbert's Barber Shop for a display, looking for residents who might want to also have the luxury in their home.

Ed Tholin and Jack Smith were former wine merchants who opened the Opera Bar in 1904. The famous photographer J.D. Wheeler opened his fine store offering oils, pastels and pictures, as well as developing film and making prints in 1907. J.W. Elliot opened Gents Furnishings and remained a prominent businessman for many years to come. In 1907, the best laundry men in town were W.E. Keeney and R.E. Dunn. The First Congregational Church built the pathway for eighty-eight local residents to enjoy service in 1893 with Reverend Chas. F. Bloomquist as the pastor.

One forward-thinking man started a brickyard in town in 1895 called M.F. Peeke & Son. After the many early and horrific fires Leavenworth endured, it stayed busy. In 1901, the population of Leavenworth was only 450, and there were no brick buildings. In 1907, there were three brick buildings: the Fritz Store, Losekamp Block and the Elliot Store. There was around one hundred homes in the area, costing anywhere from $100 to $2,000. In 1908, the population grew to around 1,500 residents, and there were nine brick buildings.

Research shows that the pioneer men traveled from all over in order to make their home in Leavenworth. In 1908, the *Leavenworth Echo* wrote full-page ads commemorating the men who made Leavenworth. Some were general merchandiser Don Thomas, who came from Wisconsin to Leavenworth in 1892, as well as Wisconsin men John Mahoney and Chas. Salick. Martin Christensen, right-hand man to Emil Frank, traveled from Colorado in 1899. The well-loved cashier at the Tumwater Bank, M.A. Marley, came from Walla Walla in 1906.

And there are a few other pioneers worth mentioning.

AMANDA C. TOWN

This courageous and high-spirited woman came to Leavenworth from Missouri in 1895 seeking better health. She had heard rumors that the climate of the Upper Wenatchee Valley could improve one's strength, so she packed her belongings and headed west.

And it worked! She soon became a restless and ambitious woman who began the first dressmaking store and millinery in town, then took to successfully managing the Leavenworth Undertaking Company. She conducted funerals, productively conducted real estate dealings and always participated in local functions. In 1920, she drove all the way to Seattle in her new car with her good friend Doctor Hoxsey's wife. That was a long and courageous task for a woman of that era.

Right: Pioneer Amanda Town came from Missouri in 1895 and fell in love with the area. She soon opened the first dressmaking shop and later managed Leavenworth Undertaking Company She was the first woman to drive through Blewett Pass, and later she flew over Leavenworth in an airplane. *Courtesy of the* Leavenworth Echo, *October 24 1919.*

Below: Thomas Goodwin sits in the driver's seat of his automobile, used as a taxi. Goodwin first arrived in the area in the 1870s to mine for gold in the Swauk and Blewett mining camps. *Courtesy of Ellensburg Library Collection.*

A favorite stopping place was the Top-o'-the-Hill Inn at the summit of 4,071-foot Blewett Pass. The large log facility offered lodging, meals, groceries, gas and oil. This photograph postcard was purchased from the Hazelwood Grocery Store in Cle Elum, Washington, owned by Albert J. Schober, an early businessman of the area. *Courtesy of Ellensburg Library Collection.*

She was also the very first woman to drive through the dangerous Blewett Pass. The pass at the time had a steep grade, sharp turns and 250 curves. And (since that wasn't enough) she later flew over Leavenworth in a plane. She could not speak highly enough of Leavenworth and was always promoting its beauty, causing several Seattle residents to make the move. She did not let the fact that she was a woman ever stop her from doing what she wanted.

Amanda was truly a woman before her time and spirited female worth noting.

DOCTOR HOXSEY

Doctor Hoxsey was a hardworking and tireless hero of the community. The amount of time and energy he offered Leavenworth is exhausting. His name crops up in article after article—Doc Hoxsey seemed to be capable of time travel at the rate he helped his local citizens. One minute he was delivering a baby, and the next he was helping at a fire or a railroad tragedy. Hoxsey came to Leavenworth (then Icicle) in 1892. He was a well-loved resident and a medical representative for the Great Northern Railroad Company. He was exposed to diphtheria, typhoid fever and many other very scary diseases of the time. For many years, he worked tirelessly day in and day out as he tended to the sick and wounded of Leavenworth. In 1906, he built a private hospital in Leavenworth to better serve his patients. During the Old Settlers Celebration in 1909, Doctor Hoxsey was considered the "most handsomest old settler" with twenty-six votes and won a box of cigars. Doc Hoxsey was even a Democratic presidential elector for the state of Washington in 1916. But one of his most celebrated and comical accomplishments was submitting the prize-winning turkey in a local contest—weighing a whopping thirty-four pounds.

A.C. BARCLAY

Barclay was a very well-respected, active and progressive citizen of Leavenworth through the years. He started out as a conductor on the Great Northern Railroad and drove trains through several section of Wenatchee and soon was called "the best known railroad man." The *Leavenworth Echo* stated on October 1, 1920, "Barclay knows every man, woman, child and dog on the road!"

In 1913, he built the Barclay Hotel located at 833 Front Street. As well as running the hotel, Barclay also ran a theater house, pool hall and auto service business. His hotel did so well that he had to add onto it an additional three-story-high section that could accommodate an extra one hundred more patrons. He would personally meet and greet every guest who came from the train and welcome them into town.

Like he wasn't busy enough, Barclay also owned a productive mine in Blewett called the Amalgamated Gold Mine. Barclay was also an accomplished motorist and was known for his speed. It was noted in the *Leavenworth Echo* on May 22, 1914, that "Mr. Barclay made the fastest time between two cities all summer! He traveled from Cashmere to Leavenworth in a mere 25 minutes flat and from Wenatchee to Leavenworth in the record time of 68 minutes!"

Today, the trip between Cashmere and Leavenworth (eleven miles) would take about fifteen minutes and the trip between Wenatchee and Leavenworth (twenty miles) would take about thirty minutes. Considering the times, Barclay really was a road racer and speed demon.

GEORGE BRISKEY

George Briskey married his bride, Mollie, in Alabama, then made the trek to the Leavenworth area and settled here in 1888. They soon had five young children and purchased a 160-acre farm. He came via Ellensburg through Blewett Pass—the pass being no more than a mere trail at that time. He built a cabin for his family where they lived happily until Mollie died in 1911. Briskey was well liked by all who knew him and was always considered hardworking and honest. They are buried side by side at the Leavenworth Cemetery.

JOHN BJORK

John Bjork is among the pioneers and one of the prominent men of Leavenworth. He moved to the area in 1891 and was by trade a contractor. Bjork and his wife never needed an introduction in Leavenworth, as they were known and liked by all who met them and had been in the hotel and restaurant business in town since 1896.

In 1904, he purchased the vacant lot that adjoined Dr. Shores Drug Store for $800. Dr. Shore had purchased the lot just three years before for a mere $75. Bjork had plans to build his restaurant on the spot. He later built the Bjork Block, which suffered from two fires—both times without insurance—the first costing $10,000 and the second costing $8,000. After all the loss from fires, he purchased over 200,000 bricks from the Hobson Brickyard for his hotel.

He leased the Overland Hotel to J.W. Elliot in 1902, when he became more interested in ranching. His building suffered the greatest loss in the big fire in 1904 that destroyed six buildings. They reopened the Overland Restaurant in 1905.

Bjork owned the Overland Hotel building until his death in 1920. He is buried at Fairview Cemetery.

10

The Unsolved Hennessy Tragedies

U nsolved murders are a shame and a horrible burden on family members. New DNA testing procedures are hard at work solving some long-forgotten crimes, finally bringing some relief to interested parties. By logging the DNA of criminals, the samples can be matched to current and past crimes, and oftentimes the criminals are already in jail and can be convicted of crimes they thought they got away with.

Another fascinating procedure police are using to solve crimes is called DNA phenotyping. This incredible new technology does not require the suspect's DNA or a match to the database but instead utilizes the DNA to create a "physical likeness of the person who left the sample behind, including traits such as geographic ancestry, eye and natural hair color, and even a possible shape for facial features."

Possibly someday the unsolved crimes involving the Hennessy Thanksgiving Tragedies can be resolved. On a bitter cold afternoon in November 1948, Gladys Hennessy was returning to Seattle from Stevens Pass after a Thanksgiving feast with her brother. She was driving home with her four-year-old son, Patrick, his dog and her best friend, Edna Gladys Horner.

As the group left Leavenworth, the snow started, and traffic slowed to a crawl. As Gladys proceeded toward Tumwater Canyon, just a few miles from Leavenworth, she hit a patch of ice, causing the car to slide sideways and fatally roll down the hill into the icy waters of the Wenatchee River.

The roads covered in ice and snow have caused many accidents. Gladys was leaving Leavenworth when her car went off the road and into the river. *Author photo.*

A man working for the great Northern Railroad stopped at the scene, as he was driving in front of Gladys and saw what had happened. Promptly, State Patrol Officer Carlson came from Leavenworth, bringing with him some volunteers and a boat. For almost two hours, their rescue efforts continued in the freezing cold. Finally, they were able to hook her car up to a tow strap, and it was pulled up from the icy water. All had been tragically killed. Her car was towed to a garage in Leavenworth for investigation.

Their Thanksgiving tragedies began in Seattle four years earlier. Gladys's husband and co-worker disappeared a few days after Thanksgiving. Earl J. Cassedy, and Gladys's husband, Seattle mortician John F. Hennessy, disappeared without a trace. They had all been enjoying a wonderful Thanksgiving dinner when another co-worker, Murphy, invited the men to his home for a drink. They drove in the pouring rain to his house and arrived around midnight, then left about 1:30 a.m. in the morning.

Neither ever arrived home that night. Both wives became worried. Finally, come Monday morning, the women feared the worst and called the police. John's wife worried that her husband, who had $260 cash on him, might have been robbed.

In order to offer assistance, the King County Funeral Directors Association offered a $900 reward for information leading to a solution to the men's whereabouts. Questionable tips poured in: someone reported gunshots toward his car on Florentia Street in Seattle and others said the men went off on a last-minute duck hunting expedition. Even other police claimed to be hot in pursuit of Hennessy's car from Monroe toward Snohomish.

Soon, the worried women received a fake note demanding $2,500 for the return of their husbands. After getting no response, they dropped the demand to a mere $500. Police launched a nationwide search party. No clues ever surfaced. No bodies were ever found.

It would be a long, grueling four years later before some resolution would finally arrive for the wives. Just before Halloween, a Seattle patrol diver stumbled upon Hennessy's car at the bottom of Lake Washington. Inside were the remains of John and Earl.

What's interesting is that police had dragged Lake Washington twice after the men vanished and went on later to thoroughly drag along the canal at every section (Lake Union, Lake Washington and Elliott Bay) but found nothing. Four years later, while divers were looking for the body of a local missing woman, they instead found the car almost one hundred feet from shore with two bodies inside.

Gladys was called with the news, and she quickly drove to the site. As they slowly pulled the rusted car from the water, she immediately identified it as her husband's automobile because she recognized an old dent in its side. The headlights and ignition switches were still on, and the gearshift lever was in put in reverse. The men were identified by their jewelry and items that could still be recognized in their wallets.

A sad note is that Hennessy's son was wearing his dad's Saint Christopher medal, the same one they recovered from his father's body when he drowned years later. The case was never solved, but some theorized that it was just a bad accident and the intoxicated men merely reversed into the icy waters.

11

OTHER NEARBY HAUNTS

A GHOST STORY FROM BRYAN S.

I spent some time working with a restaurant in Leavenworth. The owner also owned a rental on the edge of town by the gun range and the golf course. Every time I came to town they had me stay there. That place is haunted for sure. I slept with my gun under my pillow. I now believe in ghosts!

CASHMERE

In 1863, Father Respari began missionary work with the local Indians. Father De Grassi followed around 1883 and built a cabin on the Wenatchee River near the present town of Cashmere.

The first white settler, Alexander Brender, came from Germany in 1881 and filed a claim in Brender Canyon. In 1889, the Mission post office was built and John Frank Woodring established as postmaster. In 1892, a general store was built, followed by a bigger train depot in 1903 and the first brick hotel and saloon in 1905. The town, then called Mission, shared its name with several other towns, which caused confusion for the mail and train service, so the name Cashmere was officially adopted on July 1, 1904. Telephones were installed by Farmers Telephone Company in 1905, electric lights in 1914 and paved streets in 1919. The town also became a much-needed shipping point for the fruit farms nearby. An interesting note is that the telephones were only available from 8:00 a.m. until 8:00 p.m. or until the telephone operator reached the maximum wage of twenty-five dollars per month.

The *Echo* reported on December 20, 1904, that the new brick hotel was thought to be the finest on the tracks between Everett and Spokane. Two Snohomish men were granted the right to conduct a bar in Cashmere (for the outrageous license fee of $1,000) on the agreement that they would also build the hotel in Cashmere. It was required that they build a modern hotel two stories high containing at least twenty rooms.

But it was the famous Aplet & Cotlets Company that finally put Cashmere on the map. The small town has strived to replicate the American colonial period, and it is clearly one of the most beautiful small towns in Washington.

If you are searching for a little scarier paranormal activity, then drive on out to Cashmere. The town might be putting together a ghost walk for tourists, too. Cashmere also hosts a yearly event and contest called Scare-Crazy. With the support of area businesses and residences, this month-long family-friendly event displays over one hundred scarecrows, and organizers provide a walking trail map of locations.

Temptation Boutique in Cashmere

Sandy runs a wonderful shop filled with vintage clothing and jewelry, and it is located 112 Cottage Avenue in Cashmere, just a few miles from Leavenworth. She has had paranormal investigators out to her location more than a few times.

GHOST STORIES FROM SANDY

In the old days, this building was a speakeasy, and there are underground tunnels below us. They connect several of the buildings here. When I first leased this building, I was encountered by many spirits, and sometimes it was frightening. I have this area I call the "threshold" that is by the dressing rooms and the stairs that lead down to the basement. That area seems to have the most energy. I have customers who are trying on clothes and they sometimes see faces in the mirror or have their jewelry "lifted" up from their necks. I had a paranormal research team come out from the Washington State Ghost Association, and they did many investigations. The team caught many EVPs. Once they recorded "You can hear us?" Other times they captured EVPs like "What's your name?" When they asked the spirits "Why are you scaring Sandy?" The ghosts responded three times, "Friends, Friends, friends." My lights are always turning themselves off and on, we feel heavy energy now and then and customers will feel uncomfortable once in a while. I let them know that the spirits here are greeted every morning by me and asked to play nice. Dogs often can sense spirits in my building. They look up at the ceiling or choose to wait outside while their owner tries on clothes. One time, I left my keys in the door and they swayed back and forth for a really long time, too long to be normal.

I now have had the building blessed, and I do a routine every day when I enter. I say "Hello" to my shop and I say "Hello" to the ghosts and remind them that they have had all night to play around but now my store is open and they need to behave. As long as I remind them every day, the ghosts seem to understand! If not, maybe I should start charging them rent?

One time, in the basement I captured a picture of a woman with several other entities in the photograph as well as groupings of orbs. I was at the tavern by me, Club Crow, and I saw this picture of a woman. I asked, "Who's that?" The owner told me that was a picture of a former employee named Kathy who died of throat cancer two years before. It is the SAME woman that is in my photo! It is rumored that the spirits move back and forth between the buildings through the underground tunnels.

Was Kathy's ghost in Sandy's basement just wanting to talk shop with another woman? Sandy and her patrons seem more at ease now, and the ghosts keep their hauntings between 9:00 p.m. and the time Sandy's keys are heard rattling in the door first thing in the morning.

The Crow Tavern

From their website:

Our building was first opened in 1918 as a pool hall, tobacco shop and barbershop. In 1934, the first tavern license was issued to Stillman Miller, who owned and operated the tavern until 1978. The club was then purchased by Dick and Virginia Olson. The Olsons then sold it in

April of 2000 to Luke and Mary Reed. The club was then purchased by the current owners, Jack and Sheri Norris, and Tom and Paula Weedman in February of 2004, and opened for business as Club Crow on June 3, 2004. Offering some of the best local and regional blues rock entertainment, Club Crow has become "The Home Of The Blues For North Central Washington." Check out our events page and come join us for an evening of food, spirits, dancing and live blues entertainment. Club Crow is reported to be the longest still operating bar in the State of Washington.

The Crow is a must if you are craving amazing food and a great atmosphere while in Cashmere.

The Cashmere Museum

When you ask locals about ghost sightings, the Cashmere Museum comes up more times than not. It would seem logical that it would be the spirit of one very fascinating individual who had a personal challenge and dream: Willis Carey. After all his hard work and dedication, the man would never want to leave in incredible museum he created!

From their website:

In 1955, Willis Carey had a dream, he had cancer, and it was going to be a race to see which won. During his lifetime he amassed a personal collection of Native American artifacts, historical relics, antiques and curios that were famous throughout Central Washington. As his cancer progressed, he lamented to friends there was no place to house his treasures after his death. The word spread among the local businessmen and the Chamber of Commerce, led by John McDonald, began exploring the possibilities of building a local public museum for the Carey artifacts.

On a late summer day the committee visited the terminally ill Willis Carey at his home to acquaint him with the proposal. McDonald later reported that "tears of joy streamed down Carey's face" when he realized his collection might be preserved for the people of Cashmere. He immediately called for paper and pen and on the spot, signed over his entire treasure. He died the next day.

Nearly 30 years after Carey's dream was realized another addition was opened, the Russell Congdon wing with its collection obtained from archaeological sites on the Mid-Columbia. It has been called the most significant collection in the world. During the same time, a small village of original pioneer cabins was growing below the museum, preserving the rich heritage of the pioneer's contribution to the valley."

Note: The museum wishes not to be disturbed by any ghost hunters.

The Unknown Prisoner

In September 1913, a scraggly old intoxicated man was riding on train No. 4 through town. When he got off the train, he was promptly put in jail and released the next day after he sobered up. The unfortunate man then went on to purchase a bottle of liniment, which he drank. Later, he was found lying near the Great Northern railroad tracks in Cashmere in a comatose state. Doctor Martin was summoned, and the man was put back in jail. Was he trying to commit suicide? The poor man was around fifty to sixty years old and five foot, eight inches tall with no front teeth. The mysterious man was never positively identified, but several locals suggested his name was Fletcher and that he had traveled from Coulee City. Why did he come to Cashmere? Why did he want to die? If a ghostly spirit is spotted wandering near the tracks, it might be the spirit of the mysterious man from 1913.

PART II
THE GHOSTS OF THE CASCADE FOOTHILLS AND HAUNTS ALONG THE WAY

The Cascade Foothills are nestled in a plateau that was created sixteen million years ago. The area has been of keen interest for everything from hikers, gold hunters and UFO researchers to Big Foot enthusiasts and D.B. Cooper fans.

Stories of lost gold and hidden treasures seem to be the most popular. The area is rich in history and consists of thousands of acres of uncharted land.

The Cascades began to rise seven million years ago, and during that time, the Columbia River began creating the Columbia Gorge. The Cascade Mountain Range runs from Northern California through Oregon, Washington and into southern British Columbia. The Cascades are full of volcanoes, including Mount St. Helens, Mount Rainier (the highest mountain), Mount Lassen, Crater Lake, Mount Shasta and Mount Hood.

12

LOST GOLD TREASURES

Washington's Cascades are well known for their rivers and mountains being rich in gold. Washington also offers the largest number of parks that still permit metal detecting in the United States. They allow people to treasure hunt in more than thirty state parks within the area. There are several lost gold mines in the Cascades, including Rich Mine, Doukhober Mine (located in the northern part of Stevens County with its ore assayed at one thousand ounces of silver per ton) and the Pierre Rabado's Mine (thought to be located near Mount Adams in either Skamania or Yakima County). In the 1880s, Pierre Rabaldo made a gold strike on Mount Adams in the Cascade Mountains region near Bickleton. Always keeping the location a secret, he continued to prosper on numerous occasion, and Rabaldo obtained a considerable quantity of gold while there. For some reason, he never returned from one such trip in 1891, and the location of his gold mine was lost forever. It is believed that the mine lies about twenty miles northwest of Trout Lake. The hard mountainsides are still filled with beautiful and desirable treasures.

Other Cascade gold legends include stories of nuggets in Shaser Creek, ten miles south of the Stevens Pass Highway near Peshastin. Another speaks of a train accident in 1903, when gold and silver coins stashed in a safe were lost in the river below Rock Island Dam. The safe was full of treasure and never found.

Another tells of an Indian chief named Kitsap who had a secret gold mine in the Cascade Mountains. Legends say that his mine was located near the Greenwater River by Mount Rainier. The wide vein of gold was found along a steep bluff on the side of a canyon just below the snow line, as well as a large number of nuggets in the creek itself.

Many men were murdered or died trying to locate their fortune in the harsh wilderness of the Cascades. The *Leavenworth Echo* announced on September 24, 1915, "We have been shown graves, near Blewett, that owe their existence to the disputed ownership of gold nuggets. The dark tales that could be told about this old camp, before the reign of law and order began...the thimble-rigging, swindling, stock-selling and ever murders committed—all over yellow gold...would fill a book the size of ordinary law tome."

Do the spirits of these eager prospectors still protect their hidden loot, keeping them a secret to all who try to find them?

Blewett and the Peshastin River in particular were hot spots for gold. The old Blewett mining camp was located on the east side of the Cascades on Peshastin Creek, twelve miles from Blewett and sixteen miles from Leavenworth "on a good wagon road."

The *Leavenworth Echo* interviewed George Kennedy of Seattle on August 11, 1922, and found that "Amalgamated Properties had enough values both on the surface and in the veins to operate a mill grinding thousands of tons every day for over a hundred years, out of which thousands of substantial fortunes are possible...500 million tons of pay ore." This seems logical since in January 1913 it was reported in the *Echo*: "The camp at Blewett pulls ore at $12 per ton on upwards to $1,000 per ton"—motivation enough for any man who loves and desires gold to move to Blewett in search of his fortune.

Ingall's Gold

Blewett has always been known as a place rich in gold and other valuable minerals such as copper, silver and lead. In 1905, a Government Geological Report suggested that there was $2 million worth of gold in the region. The first records of discovering quartz ledge in the Blewett area actually date all the way back to 1854 by a U.S. soldier who found a vein, but the actual location was never recorded.

The legends of gold in Ingalls Creek (off Peshastin Creek about five miles from Blewett) date all the way back to 1860. As reported in the *Pioneer and*

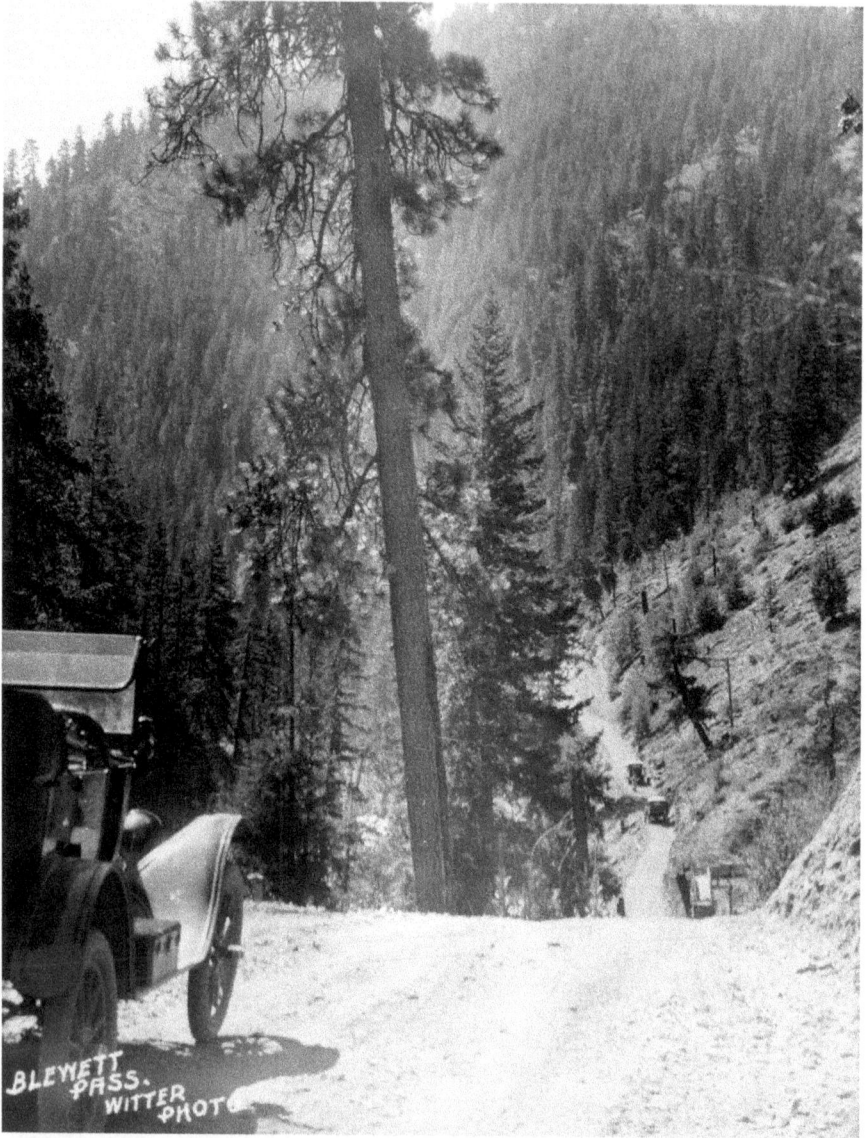

Early Blewett Pass. In 1860, gold was discovered in Ingalls Creek, sending a whirlwind of excitement all the way to Seattle. From 1860 until 1910, a whopping $1,700,000 in gold was gathered from the area. *Courtesy of Washington State Digital Archives, Blewett Pass, 1920, State Library Photograph Collection, item # AR-07809001-ph003859.*

Democrat on September 14, 1860, "Gold was discovered on Ingalls Creek by a group of about 25 miners on their way to Rock Creek....Noland & Company reported to have taken out $7,000 from Rock Creek." When the miners first found gold in Ingalls Creek, they stopped dead in their tracks and broke out their panning equipment.

The most famous gold legend is that of the Lost Ingalls gold. In 1872, Captain Benjamin Ingalls of the U.S. Cavalry accidentally became separated from his troop deep in the Cascade Mountains, so he decided to ride his mount high up the ridge of Mount Stuart to see if he could figure out where he was. Upon looking down the range, he discovered several lakes connecting below. Two of the lakes appeared deep and dark in color, but the one in the middle seemed to be a "glorious emerald green shaped like a crescent moon."

He urged his horse back down the mountain toward this particular lake. Much to his surprise, Captain Ingalls stumbled upon a huge amount of quartz loaded with ten tons of gold flecks. Excited about his discovery, he spent the next few days mapping out the area and taking samples of the quartz. Not wanting to lose his precious map, he decided to hide it under a big boulder near the mouth of the creek (now known as Ingalls Creek near Mount Stuart). He then made his merry way back to camp.

But poor Captain Ingalls never got to mine his gold fortune, as he was accidentally shot to death in 1861. The legend of his death goes that as he was traveling on horseback, the man riding behind him found a tree branch whipping toward him and it somehow managed to trigger his rifle. That misfire was the end of Captain Ingalls.

One has to wonder—was this a real accident or an unsolved murder? The story goes that before his death, Ingalls made a few unsuccessful attempts to relocate his gold. His confidant and good friend John Hansel also tried in vain to find the lost gold. Yet the Cascades were not ready to divulge the gold to anyone again.

On December 14, 1872, Washington's largest central earthquake occurred, measuring 6.8 and lasting for several minutes. During this incredibly violent earthquake, the mountains changed their shapes, geysers erupted and large boulders fell into lakes, damming the water in spots. The quake was so large it could be felt from Oregon to Canada and throughout most of Washington. The *Weekly Echo* described the incident on December 19, 1872: "The buildings in the Olympia shook until everything rattled and strained like a ship in a cyclone." The shock was reported to be so strong that it was felt in Victoria, Canada. Thousands of pounds of earth and rock

Melvin Holbrook sitting in a tree next to a canoe in which an Indian body is buried. In early days, the Indians buried their dead in trees. *Courtesy of Washington State Digital Archives, Melvin Holbrook, 1900–1920, State Library Photograph Collection, 1851–1990, item #AR-07809001-ph003109.*

crumbled—so much that it created the first dam that the Columbia River ever experienced.

The Chelan Indians called the nearby area Broken Mountain and believed that a monster spirit lived within the hills that would carry away any frightened and unfortunate men.

More stories about the legend conflict and propose other possible lakes where the gold can be found, such as the Enchantment Lakes, Leprechaun Lake, Lake Vivian and Temple Lake. Hikers tell ghost stories of spotting foggy Indian silhouettes in trees, hearing the faint shouts and cries from long-lost soldiers and even the apparition of a man on horseback dressed in period clothes.

Could this be the spirit of Captain Ingalls still searching for his lost gold or local long-gone Indians trying to protect it? No one really knows the answer. It would seem logical that an earthquake of that magnitude would certainly collapse mountains and caves, as well as hide its gold treasures to be discovered another time.

Enchantments is an area comprising an upper and a lower basin, the lakes and tarns contained within them and the peaks of the Stuart Range bounding the basins. The area is located entirely within the Alpine Lakes Wilderness about fifteen miles southwest of Leavenworth, Washington. It is considered one of the most beautiful areas in the Cascades.

THE SPANIARD'S LOST GOLD

Rumors of a rich gold mine hidden in the Cascades have been plaguing and torturing treasure hunters for over a century. Somewhere near the Lewis River between Mount St. Helens and Mount Adams there is supposed to be a gold mine worked in the late 1880s by a Spaniard. Many eager hunters tried to follow his path in order to also cash in on his find, but he was too clever to be followed. Some say he even went through the trouble of putting his mules' horseshoes on backward to confuse the greedy followers.

He would always lodge his gold in a bank in Oregon. Suddenly, the Spaniard stopped coming to the bank to deposit his gold. The legend goes that local Yakima Indians soon began paying for goods with small gold nuggets. Did they find the Spaniard's prosperous mine? Where did the Spaniard go? The Lost Spaniard Mine is said to be located somewhere between Mount St. Helens and Mount Adams, near the head of the Lewis River in Skamania County.

The skeletons of a mule and a man were discovered some years later near Spirit Lake by Mount St. Helens. Was this the body of the rich Spaniard and his faithful mule? The gold mine is rumored to be located behind a waterfall deep inside a cavern in the Cascade Mountains, and the Spaniard's restless sprit haunts the area, refusing to let anyone find and steal his precious gold.

THE EARL OF BLEWETT'S COINS AND TREASURES

The old mining town of Blewett holds another legend of lost treasure and death. There came a Scottish man named Thomas Douglas, born in Scotland in 1850 as the son of the Earl and Countess of Angus, heir to a Scottish earldom (which he somehow lost, supposedly by falling in love with a lady of lower stature), arriving in Blewett in the 1890s. He brought a chest filled with a big inheritance with him, which he buried on his property while living in Blewett and working as a miner. Legend is that he had a claim for a non-productive nearby mine called Jupiter, and he also had a passion for newspapers and magazines. Every once in a while, Thomas would board the train and head to Leavenworth to spend a few days socializing.

Locals claimed that once during a poker game, Thomas became bored and pulled a big box of coins out from under his bed. He passed the coins around, and the men drank and played cards late into the night. When Thomas again became bored, he requested all of the coins back and slowly counted them to make sure none was missing. When all was done, he sent the men promptly home.

But displaying his stash of gold was probably not the smartest thing to do, and he soon became paranoid. Thomas was seen burying his treasure in the middle of the night by a neighbor. The legend goes that one day two teenage boys stumbled on Tom's cabin, and as they peered in the windows, they saw a man lying on the floor without moving. They assumed he was dead, but just as they were turning to leave, they saw the man blink. Startled, they ran back into town to notify someone. Poor Tom had suffered from a terrible stroke, and blinking his eyes was probably the only movement he could still do to signal that he was indeed alive. He died not too long after of a stroke of apoplexy hemorrhage in March 1905. There were very few cabins in Blewett at the time of his death, and the location of his lodge is still unknown.

The cache of the coins was never found by anyone, even after many attempts to locate them. Is the ghost of Thomas still warding off any potential gold hunters from his much-loved stash of coins? When Highway US 97 was built through Blewett, most of the old buildings were destroyed, which probably included his small cabin.

Perhaps with the aid of a high-tech metal detector someone can finally find his stash of coins. Or are they forever lost and hidden under the thick, solid pavement of Highway 97?

THE HIGHGRADER'S POOR FARM TREASURE

The Hudson's Bay Company established Fort Colville in 1825. By 1859, the U.S. Army had built Fort Colville at Pinkney City. It was abandoned in 1882, and the city was moved to the present location on the Colville River Valley.

Colville was founded by John U. Hofstetter and officially incorporated on June 7, 1890.

The lost treasure of matte (a mixture of sulphides created when smelting gold) is somewhere buried near the old brickyard. Legend says that a dozen sacks of matte gold worth about $25,000 was taken from a mine in British Columbia, Canada, around 1900 and later buried near the brickyard just opposite Colville. Not much else is known about this treasure, but many have tried to find it.

13

Some of Washington's Ghost Towns

W ashington has almost sixty ghost towns for people to enjoy and numerous old mines to explore as well.

Many say the spirits of old-timers still travel the mines in search of gold. People have reported hearing the *clank, clank, clank* sounds of miners' picks hitting the hard rock and seeing the lights of a lantern late at night when no one is there. Are these spirits the ghosts from miners past still searching for valuable treasures and lost fortunes?

Early Blewett

The small town of Blewett, named after Edward Blewett of Seattle (whose mining company owned many of the claims in the area), was established around the mid-1890s due to the mining industry. It is located on the west side of Peshastin Creek in the foothills of the Wenatchee Mountains. The first claim was filed in 1874, and the bumpy road to Cle Elum was built in 1879 and another road to Peshastin in the late 1890s. The town consisted of a small school, a hotel, a few stores, a telegraph service and a saloon. In 1905, the town slowly disappeared and eventually became not much more than a ghost town. Today, the stamp mill and a few other buildings still stand.

A great example of an old building in a ghost town. The words "Ye Old Molson 1900" are on the front. *Courtesy of Washington State Digital Archives.*

Legends of lost gold and buried treasures in the area still interest and tease hunters today. Blewett Pass, Swauk Creek, Peshastin Creek and Ingalls Creek have produced about one million ounces of gold since the 1870s.

In 1892, the Blewett Company built a twenty-stamp, stream-powered mill by the mouth of Culver Gultch. Back then, the stamp mill was under the Washington Meteor Company and run by A.E. Knapp. It was the largest in the state, and Government Geological Reports stated that by 1905 the area had yielded an incredible $1.5 million in gold ore and $2 million by 1907. It was estimated that future gold from the area would produce not less than $25 million.

It was reported in the *Leavenworth Echo* on July 21, 1905, that "Blewett has great money producing value." Another fun documented fact is that Chief Joseph would water his horse and buy his supplies in the town of Blewett.

This page: The remains of the Suckling Mill in Blewett. *Courtesy of Tim Nyhus, creator of www. ghosttownsofwashington.com.*

Today, only ruins of the stamp mill, arrastra and tramway and mines remain from 1800s Blewett as fragile reminders of the town's past occupants. Some locals swear they sometimes see what appears to be the apparition of a shabbily dressed man roaming the fields late at night and swinging what looks like a pickaxe in his hands.

FRANKLIN GHOST TOWN

The little town of Franklin was established in the 1880s. Franklin had company-owned housing, a company store, a post office, a school, a Knights of Pythias hall and two saloons to serve the three to four hundred coal miners who worked the mines.

By 1891, recruiters had brought three hundred African Americans to Franklin from all parts of the United States, bribing them with good money. The white miners who were on strike due to poor working conditions were not happy about this, and fights began. Unfortunately, two men lost their lives over the quarrels. Soon, the governor requested the National Guard to restore order to the town. In 1886, Franklin residents built a post office.

Investors were interested in the Black Diamond mine in 1864, and in 1872, Leland Stanford (founder of Stanford University) opened another mine called Carbonado. In the early 1880s, fifteen shiploads full of coal were traveling from Seattle to San Francisco every month. A branch of the Northern Pacific Railroad marked Franklin as a company town, and little homes cropped up to accommodate the families of the workers. Over the first one hundred years of operations, 4.15 million tons of coal were produced from the Franklin field alone.

On August 24, 1894, the second-worst mine disaster in Washington State's history killed thirty-seven miners. Rumors switched between gossip that the tragedy was created on purpose and that of it being just a bad accident. Whatever the cause, almost forty hardworking men lost their lives that day.

Sadly, the area had one of the poorest safety records, and eighty-eight fatalities were recorded in the first four decades of mining. Almost one hundred men lost their lives pulling coal from the mountains.

Features

Cemetery, sealed mine shaft, foundations, coal cart tracks, coal cart.

Location

Follow the old railroad grade along the Green River near Black Diamond, walk up to the coal cart and sealed mine shaft and follow the narrow footpath beyond to discover the powerhouse foundation and cemetery. There are only foundations left, no buildings.

WELLINGTON (TYE) GHOST TOWN

From Bob Kelly of Skykomish Historical Society:

The only thing that I wish had been mentioned was that the railroad renamed "Wellington" to "Tye" after the disaster. They continued to operate this line for 19 years, until 1929, when the 7.79-mile Cascade tunnel under the pass was opened. Readers might enjoy visiting the Wellington site (in the summer) as it is easy to drive to by taking a side road from Highway 2 at the summit of Stevens pass. The concrete snow sheds west of Tye (Wellington), constructed after the 1910 disaster, are easily visible today on the west side of the pass from highway 2. Once you learn about this event, you will never see Stevens pass the same way again. Those railroaders from 1910 would be absolutely amazed if they could see the trains running over, or more correctly under, Stevens pass today, almost 100 years later! BNSF still deals with snow, but it is nothing like it was one hundred years ago.

Possibly one of the most fascinating ghost towns isn't a *town* anymore at all. Not much remains of Wellington except rusty scraps of the trains from the 1910 disaster buried deep down in a ravine, the eerie yet still majestic front portal of the Cascade Tunnel and, of course, the concrete snow sheds built later to deter another catastrophe.

Now a beautiful hiking trail called the Iron Goat Trail (after the Great Northern railroad logo), it remains drenched in history and, some say, the spirits of those who died on that tragic day in 1910.

A very rare photo taken inside the Bailets Hotel dining room at Wellington, Washington. Survivors of the Wellington avalanche describe remembering the checkered tablecloths in the hotel and old-timers mention Carol Thompson, who is seated on the right. *Courtesy of Skykomish Historical Society.*

As for ghosts—hikers report the cries and laughter of small children when no one is around. Others report the faint sounds of women screaming. Dogs bark aimlessly at the cold air. Young children run as if chasing and playing with other children—can they sense or see what others cannot?

A ghost story from Sue from Snohomish:

I love to hike, and I have heard such great things about the Iron Goat Trail so I decided to give it a try. I took my dog Ace with me. I always do. Anyway, we were walking along when all of a sudden I got a very eerie feeling like someone was walking up behind me. I turned around, but no one was there. It was a little creepy, and I automatically checked my pocket for my cellphone and mace. I continued to hike. It wasn't even five minutes later when the feeling came over me again. I could have sworn I heard a woman's voice crying out and I feared someone was hurt nearby. I called out. No answer. I checked my cell to make sure I had service, as I was feeling a little panicky about now. Just as I was getting to ready to head back to my car, my dog started going crazy! He's typically not a big barker, but he sure was that day! Then I heard the female voice again. I couldn't

Top: First train pulling through Wellington after the disaster and avalanche that killed almost one hundred people. Construction of the tunnel started in August 1897 and was completed on December 1900, but unfortunately it suffered from a dangerous smoke ventilation problem. *Courtesy of Leavenworth Chamber of Commerce, photographer J.D. Wheeler.*

Bottom: The Wellington Train Disaster in 1910 that killed almost one hundred people as the avalanche thrust railroad cars down 150 feet into a ravine then buried them under 40 feet of snow. *Courtesy of Library of Congress, E.J. Frazier Thompson, Montana, image 3b13980.*

really make out the words, but she sounded frightened or in pain. I couldn't take much more. I pulled on my dog's leash, and we ran back to my car. I think my dog was as eager to get back as I was! The trail is truly beautiful and maybe my imagination just got away with me, but it was an experience I will never forget.

A common experience when walking through the paths and trails is an intense sensation of compassion and an overwhelming heaviness of sadness. Psychics and paranormal investigators report a multitude of spirits that seem almost trapped in time. Are these the souls of the people who tragically lost their lives in the train wreck?

It is hard to imagine that one of the worst train disasters in U.S. history occurred right there. Almost one hundred people lost their lives during that accident, and some say they are still there waiting to be rescued. It is unknown if all the victims were recovered, as the search and rescue mission was a treacherous, bone-chilling task fought under a magnitude of snow.

The very first train coming through Cascade Tunnel. Construction started on August 20, 1897, and was completed on December 20, 1900. *Courtesy of Skykomish Historical Society.*

Century-old artifacts remain strewn about near these trails and down the ravine, the pieces littered now among the beautiful Indian paintbrush flowers, tall grasses and shrubs. The twisted metal steps that passengers once walked on while boarding the train, the mail clerks hooks and bins—all tossed into the ferns. Moss grows over trunks of the tall trees—trunks that are now entwined with cables and wires as the bark slowly grows around them, someday to cover the evidence completely.

It has been discovered that this unfortunate disaster is not known by most people. That said, before the rain and rust destroys all of the relics, or people slowly remove these items from the scene, it would be amazing if they could be preserved in a small museum commemorating those who lost their lives and those who fought to save them.

Features

Foundations, tunnel, snow sheds.

Location

Follow a path along the eastern portion of the Iron Goat Trail near Stevens Pass, once the original path of the Great Northern Railway. Visit the townsite of Wellington (later named Tye). Walk the trail east from the parking lot to see foundations of the town and the west entrance to the original Cascade Tunnel. Walk west from the parking lot to enter the snow sheds. (Please do NOT remove any items from the scene. Take only photos and memories with you when you leave.)

LIBERTY GHOST TOWN

Nestled in the Cascade Foothills south of Swauk Pass is an old mining town called Liberty (originally named Meaghersville). It is a *living* ghost town and also considered the oldest one in Washington. In 1850, it was established as Williams Creek. The first discovery of gold was in 1868 by a deaf-mute searching for water.

In the 1870s, it was the center of a Washington State gold rush and known for its large gold nuggets found among the bedrock. A surprised miner named John Black found a nugget worth $726. Another one was found near Baker Creek valued at $1,004. (In 1995, a nugget that size was worth $30,000).

C.C. Harvy cleaning and weighing gold. He sits beside a wooden building. His equipment is set on two wooden boxes, which read "KEEP IN A COOL DRY PLACE" and "HIGH EXPLOSIVES DANGEROUS," circa 1910. *Courtesy Washington State Archives, Digital Archives, Cleaning and weighing gold, 1900–1920, Martin Graf, General Subjects Photograph Collection, 1845–2005, http://www.digitalarchives.wa.gov, Ar-28001001-Ph001589.*

In 1892, a post office was established in the tiny town. Very few people still reside there, and many historic buildings and foundations can still be seen. In 1974, Liberty was added to the National Register of Historic Places. Today, many people still pan the river looking for their fortune.

In 1953, a very lucky man named Clarence Jordin Sr. hit it big at the Ace of Diamonds mine—he found a whopping 134-pound mass of gold.

Gold has been discovered in Liberty even as recently as 2013 by modern-day prospectors, and it is considered one of the best areas on Washington to try your luck. Liberty offers a unique and fascinating type of gold called "wire gold" that collectors' love. Old-timers used to pan in the valley bottoms and creeks such as Swauk and Williams.

This is a fascinating town, and the cabins are incredible and well preserved. Some of the best samples of a ghost town are here at the Williams Elliot Cabin, Jack Kirsch's cabins and the old water-powered ore mill. It is a must-see if one likes ghost towns.

The restless spirits of many old-time gold miners are probably still combing the area in search of the next big vein of sparkling and tantalizing gold.

Location

From Cle Elum, drive north on WA-970 E for about 15.5 miles. Turn right on Liberty Road. Follow about 1.5 miles.

14

RAILROAD TRAGEDIES

There were many recorded accidental deaths caused by the railroad. The railroad was, and still is, a very dangerous job. A fatal spot seemed to be near the Chumstick Bridge, with several reports of deaths caused by railroad accidents. Many of these bodies were never identified, so their names still remain a mystery.

Two deaths on the same day occurred tragically in 1904. New brakeman P.V. Ashford was killed at Nason Creek in a train accident just a few weeks into his job. On the same day, just four miles from Leavenworth, an experienced engineer named John McGourty was also killed in a train wreck by the river while working for the Great Northern Railroad.

His body was lost in the raging river. John's brother-in-law Patrick McHugh quickly came in from Chicago when he received the telegraph about John's demise. He offered a $500 reward to anyone who could find his brother-in-law's body. A few weeks later, on a bright August morning, train no. 3 was moving westbound when someone notified Conductor Shortly that they thought they saw a body in the river below. Not wanting to cause alarm, Shortly went on to Drury, detached his train and made his way back to the river. He bravely retrieved the body from the icy waters, and it was later identified as that of the missing John McGourty.

The reward soon caused commotion though, as it could not be determined who would actually claim the money. The person who first saw the body (unknown), Conductor Shortly (who retrieved the body) and the several other claimants (who claimed they also saw the body in the river)

Working on the railroad was extremely dangerous. Here a Mason County Logging Company train overturned in an accident that killed the engineer and fireman, 1914. The man to the far right is Fred Anderson, and the man to the far left is Clide Commings. *Courtesy of Washington State Archives, Overturned Train, 1914, Southwest Washington Logging and Railroad Photographs, 1914–1941, Digital Archives, www.digitalarchives.wa.gov, image Sw-28008005-Ph000005.*

all thought they were entitled to the cash. In 1912, an Indian named Dan tragically died near the same spot on the river.

During the span of years between 1897 and 1904, 62,213 people were killed and another 451,262 were injured in the United States by railroad accidents. In 1914, it was recorded in the *Interstate Commerce Commissions Bulletin* that in one quarter there were 1,624 collisions and 2,279 derailments. An interesting note is that the 1907 wage a railroad worker earned in Washington was a mere $2.16 per day.

WELLINGTON TRAIN DISASTER

Wellington was a small railroad town founded in 1893 and was originally located near the west portal of the original Cascade Tunnel near Stevens Pass.

A bleak time in Washington's history started with an intense snowfall that soon turned fatal. For nine long days, Wellington was brutalized with

The railroad rolling through a town in the Cascades in 1912. *Courtesy of Skykomish Historical Society.*

snow, as much as one foot per hour, and on one day it was stricken with an incredible eleven feet of snow.

Two Great Northern Railway trains, no. 25 and no. 27, slowly made their way down the tracks with an unexpected danger in their path. The trains' routes were delayed on the tracks near Stevens Pass, and the ever-pressing issue of heavy snow made the passengers even more nervous than they already were.

As the storm continued, they felt trapped within the metal confines of the trains—with only the eerie quiet caused by the thick, white snow that surrounded them. As the snow continued, all involved needed to determine whether it was safer to remain in the Cascade Tunnel or try to press farther on down the tracks. The rotary plows struggled to keep up with the never-ending snow. Passengers feared that if they stopped in the tunnel, they would become blockaded and suffocate in there. It was well known that the tunnel had a faulty grade and often became filled with dangerous gasses and smoke.

So the train's operator slowly pressed onward, thinking that was the best and safest route. The train consisted of half a dozen engines, fifteen boxcars, passenger cars and multiple sleeper cars. Although it had passed successfully through the Cascade Tunnel, it was forced to stop dead in its tracks near

Wellington, a small town that was filled mostly with railroad workers and their families.

Located by Tye Creek and Windy Mountain, the trains remained there as workers could not clear the tracks due to even more heavy snowfall. For six long days, the passengers and crew suffered terrible cold and edgy nerves while imprisoned inside the cars—waiting patiently and relentlessly praying to be rescued in a timely manner. Other trains were stalled in several places, as avalanches and snow continued on the long journeys between Scenic, Leavenworth and the long route to Seattle.

But their problems worsened—the telegraph lines went down, thus cutting off all communication with the outside world.

As reported in the *Seattle Star* on March 3, 1910, by passenger John S. Rogers, "The women became frantic. All day and all night you could hear trees being snapped off by the snow slides....[N]ear the train snow covered the ground at a depth of 40 feet. One gulch 50 feet deep had been completely filled with snow." Rogers left on foot with ten other impatient passengers Monday at noon. They bravely walked on foot through snow so deep the very tops of the telegraph poles barely protruded. In three hours, they courageously made it to the nearby Scenic Hot Springs.

A Great Northern Train entering the eerie, eight-mile-long Cascade Tunnel built in 1929. *Courtesy of Washington State Digital Archives, Cascade Tunnel, J.W. Thompson, 1930–1970, State Library Photograph Collection, item # AR-07809001-ph004597.*

Left: Railroad station operator Allen Batchelder in the depot at Chiwaukum, Washington, in 1918. The telegraphers "bug" can be seen on the table. *Courtesy of Skykomish Historical Society.*

Below: This photo dated October 15, 1911, shows George Edward (Heinie) Wellein at the depot operators desk in Tye, Washington. He later went on to become the chief dispatcher for the Cascade Division of the Great Northern Railway and retired with over fifty years of service. There is a mysterious woman's photograph in the background. *Courtesy of Skykomish Historical Society.*

Scenic Hot Springs Hotel. Some passengers walked to Scenic during the train stall on the tracks before the fatal avalanche in Wellington that killed almost one hundred people. *Courtesy of Skykomish Historical Society.*

Conductor Petit, who also made the trek with Rogers, was finally able to telegraph the passengers that any and all able-bodied should leave the train and head to Scenic, following the path made by Rogers and the others. When none showed up, the worried conductor fretted about the people who remained and bravely decided to make his way back to his train and its desperate passengers. Later that Monday night, thirty people were encouraged to try to also make it to Scenic, but unfortunately, they soon also became discouraged and turned back to the safety of the trains.

Little did they know that would become their final tragic fate. The snow stopped and was replaced with rain. A violent thunderstorm ensued, hitting a wide area of packed snow, causing it to crumble down the mountain. A forest fire had blazed through the area above Wellington earlier, so the damaged trees were not much help to stop the avalanche.

The terrifying and unforgettable rumble of an aggressive avalanche commencing soon was heard by anyone within earshot. And with that, on the bitter cold morning of March 1, one of the worst natural disasters in Washington State's history unfolded.

Hotel Bailets and other buildings with the railroad coming through Wellington around 1900. In 1909, the railroad upgraded the tunnel with electricity after some deaths and near misses. *Courtesy of Skykomish Historical Society.*

Snow came hurling down the mountainside, recklessly taking everything in its path. The roar of the avalanche was deafening, and its ruthless weight was said to take down telegraph poles, large trees, heavy boulders and anything else unfortunate enough to be in the way. Somehow, the avalanche missed the Bailets Hotel (and supposedly woke John Wentzel, who was sleeping inside) but smacked hard into the railroad depot.

Within seconds, both trains no. 25 and no. 27 were plucked from the tracks and forced a frightening 150 feet below into the dark ravine and into the Tye River Valley, carrying the unlucky passengers to their bitter cold fate. The railroad cars were crushed completely in several areas as they finally came to a halt against some large trees.

By then, the Scenic Hot Springs telegraph wires were completely down. The story goes that the courageous Wentzel made the frost-bitten eight-hour, eighteen-mile journey on foot in snow shoes from Wellington to Skykomish to bring horrible the news of the accident. He was so shocked and weary by the time he arrived, all he reportedly could say was "All gone. They are all gone." Efforts to pull together a rescue team quickly ensued.

After Wenzel gathered his thoughts, he told his story: "I was in Bailets Hotel in Wellington when I heard the roar....I ran outside and saw the

The Bailets Hotel and Tavern in March 1910 after the Wellington Avalanche. Photo by J.D. Wheeler with painted signage boasting Bailets as the proprietor. The incredible steepness of the mountainside can be seen in this photo. *Courtesy of Skykomish Historical Society.*

whole side of the mountain coming down, tearing up everything in its way. Trees, stumps and snow were rolling together in gigantic waves and it was going fast, terrifically fast. It was all over in less time than it takes to speak a few words."

Another hero, A.J. Mackey, bravely went out into the storm to deliver the news to others. In the dark of the night, with snow over ten feet in places, he trekked onward alone. Some thought it was a suicide mission. But Mackey was also a railroad engineer and felt a sense of duty for his comrades and the victims. James O'Neill was at the station when Mackey arrived, half frozen and exhausted. Mackey had struggled for nearly twenty hours to get to Nippon and back just to make sure the news got wired to Everett.

After the tragedy, over and over again he risked his own life in the rescue efforts for both the wounded and the deceased.

The town assembled a relief train that consisted of nurses, doctors and undertakers. As the tracks were still blocked in areas by heavy snow, the relief trains could make it no closer than Scenic, and thus rescue teams had to press onward on foot. Approaching from the east, rescue teams could get no farther than Drury, six miles east of Leavenworth, due to another snow

Left: Rare photo of the Scenic Hot Springs Hotel at Scenic, Washington, circa 1925. Lee Pickett photo. *Courtesy of Skykomish Historical Society.*

Below: Unidentified men recovering the bodies of victims from the Wellington Disaster. The building is the telegraph and cable office of Wellington. Almost one hundred people died in the avalanche. *Courtesy of Skykomish Historical Society.*

slide—one that killed a watchman named Johnson. The wounded were transported to Wellington and then moved to the big hotel in Scenic.

People gathered at the Scenic hotel during the avalanche, hoping to be rescued. It was rumored that all of the railroad and mail employees were missing. The bodies of the victims were moved slowly by toboggans to trains waiting to transport them to Everett and Seattle.

As reported by Doctor Cox, a Great Northern physician, in the *Daily Missoulian* on March 3, 1910: "110 people were tragically carried into the canyon along with 11 passenger cars, four electric motors, one rotary snow plow, one rotary shed and a sand house; all buried under 40' of snow."

The *New York Times* reported on March 8: "The day coach and smoking cars have still not been found," and "Brakemen Duncan and Conductors Purcell and Glary, who were in one of the cars that were smashed to pieces, escaped with slight bruises. In bare feet they worked for hours helping the injured and saving those caught under the wreckage."

It was later reported that the slide was a whopping half mile wide in length. Miraculously, twenty-three people survived the Wellington Disaster, but unfortunately, around ninety-six victims lost their lives. Thirty-five passengers and between fifty-eight and sixty-one railroad workers (these numbers vary) were killed that night.

The mangled railway cars from the Wellington Train Disaster, March 1910. J.D. Wheeler photo. *Courtesy of Skykomish Historical Society.*

Eight unidentified men clearing the debris and searching for victims in the harsh conditions surrounding the Wellington Disaster. *Courtesy of Skykomish Historical Society.*

Two unidentified train crew members on the depot platform at American Railway Express at the Great Northern Railroad Station in Tye, Washington, circa 1920. *Courtesy of Skykomish Historical Society.*

It took almost a month to repair the tracks. The weather was so bad that it was another twenty-one weeks later, in late July, that it was finally possible to retrieve the last of the victims' bodies from the snow.

The little town of Wellington, tired of being known only for the misfortune, wished to change its name and soon became Tye. The town was eventually abandoned, and then it burned to the ground.

To ensure no further tragedies, the Great Northern Railroad Company built nine miles of snow sheds over the tracks that ran from Scenic to Tye. For several years after the tragedy, the Great Northern Railroad spent millions of dollars to improve the area, including widening the roadbed, the erection of new and improved snow sheds (including a mile and a half of concrete sheds measuring twenty-two feet high by thirty-two feet wide running from Tye and Scenic) and a twelve-thousand-foot tunnel bored where snow sheds were not safe. These precautions were done so in the event of future avalanches, the snow would be carried *over* the moving trains.

The Wellington Depot was closed after the second Cascade Tunnel was completed in 1929. Another railroad and avalanche tragedy happened just three days after the Wellington Disaster in British Columbia, killing sixty-three people.

The Scenic Hot Springs Hotel

The Scenic Hot Springs Hotel has a fascinating history. It was originally called the Great Northern and was at McCain Hot Springs, which was developed in the late 1890s. The train station was called Madison at the time and later changed its name to Scenic.

The hot springs held almost magically healing qualities, and brochures were printed to emphasize this. Spring water was piped down directly to the hotel. The literature bragged, "No other medicinal water in the West is so effective for the cure of rheumatism, stomach, liver, bladder, blood and skin diseases!"

In 1903, two men, J.V. Prosser and George Murphy, purchased the hotel from McCain and planned to change the name to the Scenic Hot Springs Hotel. They also had ideas of increasing the patron capacity from fifty to one hundred. In 1908, the building suffered a fire. As reported in the *Everett Daily Herald*, on December 10 1909, "Hotel at Scenic Destroyed":

Scenic Hotel with railroad grading and the building of the tracks above the hotel. *Courtesy of Skykomish Historical Society.*

Scenic Hotel with railroad bulkhead and rock fill grading for the railroad in June 9, 1927. This grading is what eventually destroyed the hotel. *Courtesy of Skykomish Historical Society.*

Unidentified railroad tunnel workers along with W.E. Conroy, J.C. Baxter, C.G. Jones, Guthrie and the Great Northern Railroad Engineer McCrossan. *Courtesy of Skykomish Historical Society.*

Scenic Hot Springs Hotel caught fire last night at 7:15 pm and burned to the ground. Only one person was injured.... [I]t was finely furnished and had all modern improvements. The hotel was valued at about $50,000 and its furnishings at $30,000. A rustic room 30' x 30' was furnished with hewn logs and a large and old-fashioned fireplace that was just finished was destroyed.... [T]he engine house was the only building that did not burn. Mr. Prosser was badly burned trying to save some of his valuables. The safe had quite a deposit of servant's and guest's money and valuables. The guests and servants went to Skykomish on a freight train for hotel accommodations.

The hotel was rebuilt and reopened in July 1909 but torn down in 1929 after the railroad needed the area for its new tracks and the eight-mile railroad tunnel.

THE IRON GOAT TRAIL

In 1929, a new train tunnel was built, and the old grade became outdated and was renamed the Iron Goat Trail, which is used as a hiking trail today. Hikers can experience a trek through time as they walk through the disaster area, as some of the old ruins still remain.

A ghost story from J. Buckingham:

> *Up on Stevens Pass there's an abandoned railroad tunnel, the old Great Northern tunnel, the site of the horrific tragedy in 1910 when two steam locomotive passenger trains were swept into the canyon by an avalanche, killing about 100 people. I've heard stories of people seeing a locomotive headlight shining from the tunnel at night, and sounds of a steam whistle and screams coming from the canyon below at the old town site of Wellington (now Tye). I've heard the park rangers won't even go up to the parking lot at night while on patrol. NOT a place to be after dark!*

Many pedestrians have reported a very creepy feeling as they use the trail. Perhaps the ghosts of the 1910 passengers still linger, destined to their tragic fate forever, wishing to haunt those who pass by them going about their day. Most people have not even heard of the Wellington Disaster, so maybe the spirits wish to communicate in the hopes of not being entirely forgotten?

Location

The old Iron Goat Trail can be found by traveling Highway 2 to milepost no. 64.3 just past the Stevens Pass Summit. Then, turn onto the Old Cascade Highway, next turn onto Forest Service Road 050 after you go 2.8 miles. There also is an interpretive site at milepost no. 58.3 on Highway 2, just 10 miles east of Skykomish. The Iron Goat Trail is approximately two hours northeast of Seattle. Please do not remove any of the historic relics so others can experience and appreciate the trail, too. There are only two structures left that were in place at the time of the disaster: the west portal of the Cascade tunnel and the concrete walls. A small concrete block structure is located at the point of the old Haskell Creek bridge. This road is not open during the winter.

ANOTHER RAILROAD GHOST

Railroads still hold a certain charm and mystique, as one can fantasize about the old days when boarding a train was a rare, fascinating and exciting journey. Possibly a new romance would arise after a few hours boarded, or several hands of poker might make one a little richer and pockets a little heavier than when they left the depot.

One well-repeated haunting was told by a railroad engineer named J.M. Pinckney in 1892. He was traveling on Northern Pacific going eastbound through the Cascades, comfortably en route in the main engine car with the conductor and fireman. The men passed the time by eagerly swapping tales of horrible train wrecks, overturned boxcars, tragic accidents and so on. This storytelling went on for some time until suddenly the conductor, in a panic, grabbed the throttle and reversed the engine. The high-pitch screeching sound of air brakes filled their ears as the train came to a shuddering stop.

He had stopped the train within just feet of the very spot where Engineer Cypher had met his death just two years prior. The conductor acted like it was nothing and soon moved his train back into motion. Curious passengers began asking, "What was the matter? What made them suddenly stop?"

Pinckney was not fooled by the conductor's casual attitude and lame excuse, as they had known each other for a long time. After a few more moments of travel, a man yelled, "There! Look there! Don't you see it?"

Pinckney, upon looking up, also saw the lights and felt panicked, fearing a violent collision. But after a few moments, the conductor casually moved on, calmed down by now.

When asked why he wasn't stopping the train to avoid a collision, he answered, "Oh, it's nothing. It's what I saw back at the Gorge. It's just Tom Cypher's engine No. 33….Have I seen it before? Yes, 20 times. Every engineer running this road knows that ghost engine, and always watching for it when he gets to the Gorge."

The men remained calm but unsettled. They could clearly see the engine ahead of them and the faint sight of smoke coming from the caboose. At one point, they thought they could even see a figure on the train standing at the gears.

Could it be the ghost of Tom Cypher relentlessly continuing to run his train route along the Cascades?

A Deadly Spot on the Tracks

Coincidences happen, but sometimes the chances are too slim to ignore. Just outside of Leavenworth there was a mysterious spot on the train tracks that led to several deaths. A segment of the tracks appeared to be paranormal or jinxed. Ghosts may become trapped at a location because of a tragic accident, suicide or some other negative energy.

In the case of this particular area of tracks, two railcar accidents happened within a few weeks of each other in the exact same spot. Coincidence or something more mysterious?

On May 23, 1907, over one hundred yards of track were torn up, possibly by a broken wheel. An unfortunate diner car worker was killed, and his assistant was badly injured, as were a number of passengers. The diner car, day coach and two sleepers were completely overturned, becoming a mangled twist of metal. Mere weeks later, on June 4, the *Wenatchee Daily World* reported yet another fatal train wreck in the same spot.

This time, a well-known Leavenworth man named Clyde Cahale and his co-worker for the Great Northern were traveling eastbound on train no. 4 when around 10:00 p.m. it derailed because a huge boulder was in the middle of the tracks. Unable to brake quickly enough, Fireman Clyde was forced to jump from his engine. Unfortunately, he was on the river side. Cahale's body was never found, and many feared it was washed down the Wenatchee River or trapped under the wreckage. His fellow engineer, McKay, jumped out on the land side and was saved.

Engine no. 4 may just have had bad luck, but two years prior to its June 4 wreck, it jumped track in in the same spot, killing one of the company's best men, McGourty, as it plunged into the icy river.

Why would one small area out of thousands of miles of track cause three deaths and three wrecks?

The 1904 Disastrous Wreck

Possibly the same area where the phantom train paranormal episodes occur, the Chumstick Bridge has had its share of tragedies.

Late one night in 1904, an eastbound passenger train went into a ditch off the bridge. The bridge was built on a dangerous curve 100 feet above the Wenatchee River. On this fateful day, Engineer Croak and Fireman Wilson

Engine and Rotary Plow wreck in Leavenworth on February 27, 1916, near Tumwater Canyon. *Courtesy of Skykomish Historical Society.*

A train loading coal. *Courtesy of Ellensburg Library Collection.*

were riding along when Jack Croak commented on how he could "feel the ground giving away." Just seconds later, a 250-foot section of the road bed gave way and quickly slid down into the icy river, taking the engine, the mail cars and the passengers cars tumbling along with it.

During the rescue, three men were instantly killed, as they were riding on the front end of the mail car without permission. One of the three men was later identified as F.J. Wildman, a member of the Tribe No. 15 of the Red Men and member of the Painters Union in Montana. The other two bodies were never identified.

Croak and Wilson were rushed to Doctor Hoxsey and treated in the hospital. Both men were badly injured. Wilson recovered, but Croak unfortunately died that night in his sleep.

Miraculously, Croak's eight-year-old son survived the accident. Just prior to the wreck, when the train entered Leavenworth, he had asked his father if he could join him in the engine room. Croak, knowing it was too dangerous, told his son to go back and stay in the mail car.

Did Croak's intuition let him know something bad was going to happen? Did listening to his intuition actually save his son's life? Croak was a well-loved individual and had been working for the company for over twenty-five years.

In 1903, a dozen train cars wrecked just two hundred feet from the 1904 incident. It is a haunted spot on the old railroad tracks, for sure.

15

HAUNTED HOTELS

THE SKYKOMISH HOTEL AND BUSH HOUSE HOTEL

SKYKOMISH

Skykomish is an old railroad town that is a favorite spot to stop on the way to Stevens Pass or Leavenworth off Highway 2. In its day, it bustled with workers and activity and was the home to several thousand people. It is hard not to fall in love with the town if you are a history junkie.

With the boom of the Great Northern Railroad in 1893, workers decided to settle down in the area surrounding the area where the trains would stop to refuel. Skykomish pioneer John Maloney, at age thirty-three, moved to Seattle from Alaska. He secured a job with the Great Northern Railroad to determine a route over the seemingly impossible Cascades.

Maloney wasn't deterred by complications, and construction on the railroad began in the fall of 1890. Moving to Skykomish, he then built a post office and general store. The store is now located to the left of the Skykomish Hotel on the corner of Fifth and Railroad Avenue. It has a fancy western façade and originally was only thirty by sixty feet in size. It is listed in the National Register of Historic Places and the Washington Heritage Register. His land plat in 1899 was between the river and the train tracks.

In 1909, when the Scenic Hot Springs Hotel caught fire and burned to the ground, its guests and servants went to Skykomish on a freight train for hotel accommodations. They probably stayed at the Skykomish Hotel.

Main Street of Skykomish with the Maloney General Store, Hotel Skykomish and the saloon. John Maloney was the town's founder, and he built the store in 1893. *Courtesy of Skykomish Historical Society.*

Four unidentified people enjoy spending time with a horse on the front portion of the Skykomish Hotel. *Courtesy of Washington State Archives Skykomish, 1965–1968, Werner Lenggenhager, State Library Photograph Collection, 1851–1990, Digital Archives, www.digitalarchives. wa.gov., image #AR-07809001-ph001279 and Skykomish Historical Society.*

During the Wellington train disaster in 1910, John Wentzel stopped in Skykomish to tell them of the train wreck and tried to pull together a rescue team. He probably walked into the Skykomish to tell of the bad news.

Skykomish, always being a generous and caring town, also helped during another tragedy. In July 1922, a fire broke out in the nearby town of Tonga. The sawmill caught fire, causing a loss of $150,000, and the citizens lost everything. A section of the railroad tracks was also destroyed. A special train was loaded with the women and children of Tonga and carried to Skykomish to be well cared for by its citizens.

Skykomish is rich in history and is a beautiful and interesting town filled with friendly and supportive people. The community is tightknit and progressive in its plans to improve the town every year.

The Skykomish Hotel

One cannot drive into the little town of Skykomish and miss the Skykomish Hotel. It stands four stories tall and appears massive in consideration to the buildings around it. It was built in 1904 (on the same site as another hotel that had burned down) by a man named Manning, and it cost him $10,000. Many patrons of the railroad stayed at the Skykomish Hotel on their travels, as it was considered a local favorite.

Later, in 1935, Manning left the hotel to his daughter and son-in-law, Curtis and Anna Manning Brotherton. Earl Riddle purchased it in 1944 and sold it to Bill Roberts in 1965. In the 1960s and '70s, the hotel was called Molly Gibson's, and it featured a bar with live music and dancing. This was a very popular stop for skiers going to Stevens Pass. In 1979, Bill and Chris Dieffenbach took over ownership and renovated much of the bottom floor. Don and Gerriann Flynn purchased the hotel in 1989 and sold it to Adam Dopps and Jane Lenzi in 1997 but received the hotel back a few years later. In 2000, the Flynns sold the hotel to Karl Benz. During this time, the hotel deteriorated to its current state. Extending north, a one-story wing that once contained a bar and banquet room collapsed and was later demolished in 2009. Neglected and in disrepair, the roof no longer protected the building from the elements, and rainwater was allowed to damage the interior of the building for over a decade.

Today, it is being remodeled in the hopes of returning it to its former glory. A cumbersome and expensive task, it has been gutted down to the

As of 2017, the Skykomish Hotel currently is undergoing major renovations. Remodeling is said to awaken spirits, and many paranormal groups have investigated the hotel with very scary findings. *Author photo.*

studs and required a new roof and foundation. Everyone in town is excited to have the gorgeous hotel being restored to its former glory.

As for ghosts, it is said to be the home of the blue lady. The story goes that on the very top floor of this place there used to be a speakeasy, where the ladies of the night entertained and where gambling went on. One of the prostitutes had taken up with a new man. The boyfriend walked in on her as she was doing business with a john. He was so enraged he killed her. Previous owners and paranormal investigators claim to be contacted by her sad and lonely spirit. She can be seen wearing a light-colored negligee at times, perhaps in the hopes of entertaining a few men?

When the hotel was up and running, workers claimed they could hear the sounds of glassware and silverware clanking even when no customers were in the restaurant. There are also rumors that a customer from the old days killed a prostitute in room 32 and her ghost refuses to leave the room.

There are many claims that the lights turn off and on by themselves, too. Although with a building this old, wiring problems may be at fault.

Skykomish Hotel with crowd of unidentified people during a city celebration. Notice the muddy streets and planking of the times. *Courtesy of Skykomish Historical Society.*

When the building is remodeled, if the lights continue to do this, then it appears that it might be her restless spirit trying to get some attention. When you stop in Skykomish, you can peek in the windows and get a sense of what the hotel must have been like in its former days. It is a little creepy as you peer through the dusty old windows, going back in time just a bit.

Paranormal investigators have witnessed and recorded many EVPs, and several felt the sensation of being touched by unseen hands.

Skykomish School

This school was constructed in 1936 and replaced an older two-story wood schoolhouse. It has strived to harmonize both historical attributes as well as functionality. Not to frighten any current students, but some locals claim it can appear to have a friendly spirit or two.

A ghost story from a local citizen:

It was nice meeting and speaking with you a couple days ago, as I said I was going to get a story or two from my kids about their encounters with the paranormal at Skykomish School. The first one was last year in the gym waiting to start P.E., my son was a part of the class at this time and stated that while waiting there was a crash up in the balcony area, like something had fell down; however, there is nothing stored up there nor was there any person.

The next two stories occurred in the girls' bathroom. My daughter was in there when she heard the door open and close and nobody came in. The second time her and her friend were in the bathroom at the sinks, when they heard the stall doors open and close and they were the only two people in the bathroom.

INDEX

Bush House Hotel

The Bush House in Index, on the way to Leavenworth from the west, has many legends, stories, rumors and gossip surrounding its crumbling walls. In 1893, the town of Index was platted by Amos and Persis Gunn on their mining claim. In 1897, the Sunset Mine, located five miles east of Index, hosted large amounts of copper, which made the town's economy flourish. The Bush Hotel was built in 1889 for the local miners, and Index was once a thriving town for tourists.

In the good old days, the Great Northern Railroad actually stopped in Index at the Bush House Hotel, and passengers found themselves being warmly greeted by Mrs. Bush herself.

The hotel went through many owners. It needed many repairs over the years and even suffered an earthquake in 1999. In 2002, it officially closed its doors.

Vandalism soon took its toll on the historic building, destroying the walls and the beautiful interior glass, making locals nervous. Luckily, new owners and Index residents purchased the once gorgeous hotel and began eagerly making costly repairs and renovations. They have created rooms to support the local history of the town through photographs, period pieces and relics from the era.

The ghostly legends surrounding the Bush Hotel include the story of a young future bride named Annabel who came to Index to wed her coal miner fiancé. There was a tragic explosion at the site he worked, and poor Annabel, distraught with grief, hanged herself in room 9. Unfortunately, her

Above: The Bush House Country Inn located in Index was established in 1898 and is believed to house several spirits. After being vacant for some time, it is currently being renovated as a beautiful venue for generations to enjoy. *Author photo*.

Right: Seven unidentified men posing with the first car, a Flanders 20 model Hupmobile, to reach Index in the spring of 1911. The team is parked in front of the Bush House Hotel and went on to Galena despite the fact there were no real roads at the time. *Courtesy of Skykomish Historical Society*.

Bush House Country Inn is said to house a ghost named "Alice" who reportedly heard her husband had died. In despair, she unfortunately hanged herself in room 9, although her husband was later found alive and well. *Courtesy of Skykomish Historical Society.*

fiancé was not one of those involved in the disaster. The rumor is that he was so distraught with sorrow that he, too, killed himself after he found her dead. A new-age Romeo and Juliet, the two lovers are said to still roam the halls of the hotel. Footsteps, crying, cold rushes of air, lights always flickering and rearranged furniture are just some of the paranormal activity said to happen at the hotel.

A ghost story from Aaron in Monroe:

> *My friend's mom's friend used to work at the old Bush Hotel when she was young. She said she heard a voice say "Hello, are you cleaning my room?" Things moved without anyone moving them. Weird sounds for no reason. Doors opening and closing by themselves. It is rumored that a woman hung herself there a long time ago. Other locals say that kids played on the tracks and one got killed. Sad.*

There are many other legends of the Bush House Hotel that include seeing people looking out through the curtains when no one is inside, lights flickering when the building is vacant and rumors of a suicide from the high terrace area, as well as odors of flowers in the halls in the dead of winter.

Location

The Bush House Inn is located in Index, Washington, at 308 Fifth Street, just one mile off of Stevens Pass Highway (Highway 2), just one hour from Seattle, thirty minutes to Stevens Pass Ski/Board and one hour from Leavenworth. The historic inn is within walking distance of nationally acclaimed climbing and hiking areas; rafting, kayaking and fishing on the Skykomish River; and snowboarding, skiing and snow-shoeing at Stevens Pass. It is a five-minute drive from Reiter Foothills Park, known for its off-road vehicle course and single-track and mountain bike trails. The Bush House Inn is the perfect place to stay and play. In addition to historic-themed accommodations, the inn will contain a bakery, restaurant and bar. It is currently under renovation and will open soon. Visitors are asked to remain outside the construction area for safety reasons.

MERRITT HOTEL

The little town of Merritt was known as a local favorite spot to camp, hunt and fish but also had other positive attributes.

Locals and investors decided to open a talc mine near the railroad just west of Merritt. The valuable talc would be shipped to the coast, where it would be used in the manufacturing of paint and paper products.

In 1906, Merritt provided even more interest to people, as a man stumbled upon a wet bog that proved to be of high-grade kerosene oil. Soon a three-thousand-foot well was being drilled, and a dozen claims were staked out. The profitable oil was found just half a mile from the post office by Nason Creek Valley.

In 1907, a man named H.B. Smith from Ohio met with surveyors and camped in the lovely location of Merritt. The railroad would soon be building a depot there as well. In 1909, Smith became the hotel keeper and postmaster. It was rumored he would never return to Ohio because he found the area of Merritt so beautiful. In 1910, the town was actively promoting itself along with Tumwater Canyon with train excursions to the hotel, where the proprietors served a fabulous dinner that ended with free berries and ice cream to patrons.

But the summer of 1909 brought a personal tragedy to Smith amid all his endeavors. His friend and local well-liked prospector Samuel Hawkins was

The Hotel Merritt and General Store was located along Highway 2 at the Great Northern Railway station east of Stevens Pass at Merritt, Washington, 1911. The hotel is gone, but the sleepy village is still home to railroad activity. *Courtesy of Skykomish Historical Society.*

accidentally killed by an eastbound freight train while walking home late one night. Hawkins had come to Merritt to visit friends and purchase groceries and supplies. He then began the long trek to his small cabin about eight miles from Merritt. At this time, the snow was an incredible fifteen to twenty feet high on each side of the tracks. Hawkins was walking in the area of the tracks, as they had been cleared of snow. He was on his way home when he heard the sound of a train moving toward him. Panicked, he quickly tried to climb the icy slopes to get out of the way of the train.

But Hawkins could not get out of the way fast enough, and he was killed instantly. He was one of the best-known gold prospectors in the county. Hawkins and Smith were supposed to team up on finishing a 150-foot-long tunnel on his property just west of Merritt. Hawkins was sixty years old when he died.

In the summer of 1911, the hotel went though some more changes, as Smith was temporarily relieved by Curtis Mann, from Aberdeen, who took on the role of hotel proprietor, postmaster and store keeper. Mann wanted to improve the hotel, as it was considered one of the most popular places to

The Hastings Store was located at today's Nason Creek rest area along Highway 2, west of Leavenworth. The store served a small farming community that also included the Dardenelles Post Office and the Great Northern Railway station of Nason Creek. *Courtesy of Skykomish Historical Society.*

visit and entertained hundreds of visitors each summer. Smith took a passion to gardening with some well-deserved time off and entered his vegetables in several local contests along with his gardening rival H.S. McNett. Smith was awarded first prize by the Leavenworth State Bank for the best half bushel of potatoes, with McNett coming in second place. The Leavenworth Mercantile Company was awarding the prizes for the best three heads of cabbage, and Smith and McNett went neck and neck again—but Smith won first. McNett did not go away empty handed, though, as he won first place in the best onions contest.

By summer 1912, Smith had bought the hotel back from Mann, and it was officially reopened to the public that summer and boasted an open-air dancing pavilion with a large dance floor. Train no. 44 could take patrons right to the hotel from anywhere. Those who wished to drive an automobile were encouraged to do so, as the new road from Wenatchee to Merritt had just been completed a week before at a cost of $2,000 per mile.

In January 1913, Merritt endured an exhausting ten feet of snow that rose up to fourteen feet in some spots. Proprietor H.B. Smith was not discouraged,

These brave men work a rotary snow plow through almost thirty feet of snow on the tracks. The winter of 1915–16 recorded one of the heaviest snowfalls in the history of Washington. *Courtesy of Ellensburg Library Collection.*

and he wished to invest $50,000 in the hotel and new summer resort in town. He also wanted to build hiking trails that led to the nearby lakes for future patrons to enjoy.

But in July, tragedy struck the hotel, as it went up in flames at ten o'clock one evening. Being made of wood, the hotel burned quickly to the ground, and little was able to be saved. Smith estimated his loss at $6,000 and (just as many business owners at that time) did not have adequate insurance to cover the full amount. Smith was still determined to rebuild the hotel by the following summer. He was the county's biggest promoter of the Cascade Scenic Highway and was constantly working on improving the roads. One year, he even raised a whopping $5,000 to be used in its construction.

Smith engrossed himself the following years with the very important construction of the Cascade Scenic Highway and took charge of the Chelan County's portion of the road. In 1914, it was recorded that Chelan County collected $106,296.76 in just one day in taxes—with $94,125.21 coming directly from the Great Northern Railroad in a single check.

16

THE MINE TRAGEDIES

THE CITY OF ROSLYN

Roslyn is located in the eastern portion of the Cascade Foothills, founded by a courageous and energetic young man named Logan Bullitt, who worked for the Northern Pacific Coal Company. In 1886, Bullitt came to acquire his fame and fortune—and hopefully the love of a beautiful young lady named Roslyn.

In her honor, the town officially became named Roslyn on August 10 that same year. In 1888, Roslyn officially incorporated as a city in Washington Territory, but the celebration was thwarted by a ferocious fire that broke out on Second Street that quickly burned down the entire business district.

The citizens of Roslyn were determined and unwilling to walk away from their town, so they gathered resources and rebuilt the town in the summer of 1889. The small town hit a boom when the Northern Pacific Railroad (Northern Pacific Coal Company was also part of the Northern Pacific Railroad) took interest due to the amount of coal the town housed deep beneath its surface. Although the coal business flourished, the miners became disgruntled with their poor working conditions and low wages, so they went on strike. Soon, three hundred African American men were shipped into town by a man named James Shepperson. These workers had no idea that they were part of a tense strike.

Racial tension, fistfighting and possible bloodshed were feared among the locals and their families. Yet the simple need of a schoolhouse in Roslyn brought the two races together peacefully in a sense of community. The black citizens kindly offered their church to the town as the site of the much-needed school. The racial tension and any resentment were lifted, and slowly, they all worked together for the common good of the town.

The population quickly zoomed from a few hundred to an incredible four thousand people during the late 1920s. But in the 1960s, the last coal mine closed, and the town threatened to become yet another Washington ghost town. The town again became predominately white, with a mere one thousand residents. By 1970, only a single black family remained in town, and in 1976, William Craven became the first black mayor in the state of Washington.

ROSLYN MINE DISASTERS

A Horrible Accident

The prosperous small town soon developed the Roslyn Mine No. 1, and it grew back up to 1,200 residents by 1886. Due to the fact that the railroad needed coal to fuel the locomotives and this area had plenty of coal, men worked hard to build the railroad that would soon spread from Cle Elum to Roslyn, and little homes sprouted up along the tracks. All was going well—in fact, so well that three more coal mines blossomed nearby.

There was so much coal that Mine No. 1 quickly grew into seven deep layers that went a frightening 2,700 feet below the town's surface. Ventilation was poor despite almost a dozen furnaces burning 24/7 to create drafts. Methane gas would build up in the tunnels, making very dangerous working conditions for the men. At the time of the explosion, workers were trying to build a new passage near the fifth level into the sixth to improve the air flow.

And that was when the most feared incident for Roslyn's citizens would soon happen. On May 10, 1892, a horrendous fire broke out in Northern Pacific Coal Company's No. 1 mine, causing an unexpected, terrible and fatal explosion. An incredible explosion from deep inside the mine that shook the earth. Hearts soon sank as people above ground and nearby knew the men would not be able to get out of the tunnels in time to save their own lives.

Later it would be determined by First District coal mine inspector David Edmunds that the explosion was detonated by some blasting powder that

Above: The Roslyn mine's warehouses and shops can be seen, as well as old piles of culm (waste coal). *Courtesy of Washington State Digital Archives, Aerial view of Roslyn mine, 1948–1955, State Library Photograph Collection, item #AR-28001001-ph000436.*

Left: Coal mining was a very dangerous job with bad conditions, and many brave men lost their lives working the mines. *Courtesy of Washington State Digital Archives, Coal Miners at work, 1945–1955, State Library Photograph Collection, item #AR-28001001-ph000444.*

A very dangerous mining tunnel near Roslyn, Washington, in September 1939. Running down the tunnel are railroad tracks. *Courtesy of Washington State Archives Coal Mining Tunnel, 1939, Ed Juris, General Subjects Photograph Collection, 1845–2005, Digital Archives, www. digitalarchives.wa.gov., image #AR-28001001-ph000423.*

was used to break up the rock. The mining blast opened a crack to a pocket of gas, and a miner's lamp on the slope side set off the explosion.

It was quickly recorded as the worst coal mine disaster in Washington's history. The dangerous and incredible rescue efforts started immediately, and fourteen bodies were soon pulled from the mine on the first day. Three days later, they were finally able to recover all forty-five bodies. Nearby towns did not hesitate to help the town in its time of need—food, clothing and labor were offered from hundreds of caring citizens. Almost thirty widows mourned their losses, almost one hundred orphans were created and many families were devastated by the disaster as the putrid smell of smoke filled their lungs for days afterward. The bodies of the deceased were buried in the nearby cemetery—of course, segregated by their skin color. Some filed lawsuits against the Northern Pacific Coal Company, and it settled for $1,000 to each widow. But if a widow had a "working age son," she received only $500 for any inconvenience.

Over 50,000 miners lost their lives working the coal between 1870 and 1914. That amounts to 1,136 deaths per year or 3 deaths per day. It was considered one of the most dangerous jobs to do, other than working on the railroad.

Another Roslyn Mining Tragedy

It was another sad day indeed on Sunday October 3, 1909, in the small town of Roslyn, Washington. An awful explosion took the lives of almost a dozen hardworking men. This tragedy occurred just seventeen years after Washington State's worst mine disaster ever, which claimed the lives of forty-five miners.

This day in October, around noon, an explosion rang loud in Mine No. 4, taking ten men with it. The small buildings near the shaft were also destroyed.

The rescue party went into the mine via No. 1 in an attempt to reach the bottom, but it was blocked. Out they came and tried No. 2. They were only about three thousand feet into the mine when several of the men became ill and had to resurface. Multiple other attempts were made, but rubble and cave-ins made their efforts impossible.

Almost giving up hope, the men waited patiently for men from the U.S. Geological Survey crew arrived to offer assistance. This was on October 8, five long days after the explosion. The men carried state-of-the-art helmets and equipment as they entered the shafts. They were able to find a pumpman named Jones, but he was deceased. Scarce ventilation threatened their equipment and the lamps, making the rescue complicated. They carried no modern-day flashlights or electric lamps, and the threat of gas disturbing their safety lights loomed over their heads.

The next night, seven men entered again and found two more bodies, then another few more men were discovered fifty feet from where they were working. The rescuers found many collapsed areas in the tunnels. In fear of another possible explosion, they shot water down the shafts to prevent fire and calm the dust. For almost two days, the water ran to settle the dust and smoke.

That very morning the mine was inspected and was within normal limits. It was determined later that the cause of the explosion was a probably a dust explosion.

The last Roslyn coal mine closed in 1962, bringing an end to the long and dangerous task of coal mining for the town. Some locals talk of wandering and restless spirits that roam late at night, still in shock from the mining tragedy. Sometimes some say the faint smell of burning coal lingers in the midnight air.

MORE ROSLYN HAUNTS

The Old Roslyn School House

The spirits of students past appear to not want to leave the Old School House in Roslyn. Local stories consisting of writing instruments moving on their own, locker doors opening and closing without the assistance of a human and even toilets flushing by themselves are all reported to occur in this old haunt.

The Brick Saloon

The Roslyn Brick Tavern, or Brick Saloon, is known for its haunted past, but the current owner would like nothing to do with ghosts and spirits—except of the *bottled* kind. (Please be respectful of the owner's wishes to ignore any ghosts and/or hauntings.) Another tidbit about Roslyn: it was the setting for the 1990s TV series *Northern Exposure* and previously for the film *The Runner Stumbles*, starring Dick Van Dyke in the late 1970s.

In September 1889, partners John Buffo and Peter Giovanni opened a tavern in this very location. The tavern was later rebuilt in 1898 using forty-five thousand bricks and obviously took the new name the Brick Saloon. Its fabulous back bar is one hundred years old and was purchased in Portland, Oregon. It originally came from England and still has a curious twenty-three-foot running water spittoon.

It is claimed that the Brick Saloon is the oldest operating saloon in Washington State. As for ghost stories, rumor has it that the building was once a jailhouse, but others claim the cells were just part of the film production. Some see a little girl running around the tavern at odd hours; others claim to see a cowboy figure. Previous workers have told locals of hearing a piano playing, laughter when no one else is there, the sounds of glasses clanking and even the faint whiff of a tobacco pipe.

Location

From I-90 east or west, take exit 80 (Roslyn and Salmon La Sac) onto Bull Frog Road. At the second roundabout, follow signs to Roslyn via SR 903. Turn left onto Pennsylvania Avenue. The Brick is located on the corner of SR 903 and Pennsylvania Avenue. (Please respect the owner's wishes to not be bothered with the paranormal.)

A NEARBY MINE TRAGEDY

Franklin Mine Disaster

In 1885, the Seattle and Walla Walla Railroads were extended from Black Diamond to Franklin, thus allowing shipments of coal to be sent to San Francisco. On August 24, 1894, the worst mine disaster in King County history occurred at the Oregon Improvement Company mine in Franklin. A fire caused thirty-seven miners to suffocate in the mine.

A jury later found that the fire had been intentionally set, but the person responsible had also perished in the disaster, never to be legally prosecuted for his actions.

There are no buildings left, just foundations, no residents. The cemetery is the primary clue to finding this ghost town.

17

OTHER MYSTERIOUS PLACES

ELLENSBURG

Ellensburg is known for its rodeos, but the town located in Kittitas County offers a lot more than that. The history of Ellensburg began in January 1873, when the gold rush moved into the one-thousand-acre Swauk Creek area. In 1871, John and Mary Ellen Shoudy claimed 160 acres, and he named the town after his wife and built the first two-story building. Soon the couple built a trading post named Robber's Roost. The city of Ellensburg was first incorporated on November 26, 1883.

In the summer of 1887, the Northern Pacific Railroad completed its tracks across the Cascades, which would finally connect Ellensburg with the nearby Puget Sound area. Ellensburg blossomed, and the first telephone in town was installed in the fall of 1889. The first auto made its way across the Snoqualmie Pass in January 1905, making headlines. All this comes to the wonderful accomplishment of Ellensburg's first rodeo on September 13, 1923. Little did they know Ellensburg would enjoy many profitable and enjoyable rodeos for all its years to come.

THE OLD OLMSTEAD PLACE

Now a beautiful state park and museum, the history of the Olmstead House began in the late 1800s. The old homestead was once used as a Native American fort. Tourists report of the sense of being watched, and some have even said they have seen apparitions of Indians on the land near the creek. Others report the sounds of a woman and baby crying. Indians in the area were very spiritual people, and the men of the tribe used the sweat lodge to increase spiritual awareness; cleanse the spirit, body and mind; remove evil spirits; prepare for hunts; and for coming-of-age events. A fire was built around rocks hours before the lodge was used and then water was slowly dripped on the very hot rocks to create steam. The lodge was tightly sealed to prevent the steam from escaping, enhancing the experience.

A ghost story from Sue Q. from Snohomish:

> *I love museums and historic homes. When my husband and I came across the Olmstead State Park near Ellensburg, we decided to stop. It is a little eerie to see all that old stuff right in its original place—like time had stopped. It reminded me of when my dad died and the first time I went to visit his house. His razor was still on the sink, his coffee cup still on the counter, his laundry still in the washing machine...it hit me so hard. I even had the weirdest thought, "Dad will never eat pickles again," as I was clearing out his fridge and was throwing things out. My dad loved pickles. Anyway, my husband and I were roaming the park—it's really beautiful—and when we visited the old house I could have sworn I saw a female figure in the kitchen area and the faintest whiff of bread baking. They say that ghosts can create certain smells. I wondered if Sarah Olmstead was still hanging around her old farm, baking bread for her family. It was a very pleasant thought!*

In 1875, the Olmstead family braved their way on horseback across the treacherous Snoqualmie Pass in the hopes of building a life in this new territory. They decided on an area just outside of the beginning of what is now called Ellensburg, where the land was fertile and water was plenty being provided by the nearby Coleman and Altapes Creeks. Mr. Olmstead began chopping down the cottonwood trees in order to construct a small cabin for his family. With the help of his wife, Sarah, they were able to create a beautiful farm that would stand the test of time for many years to come.

The Smith sisters, Clareta and Leta May, were born in the late 1880s on the Olmstead Ranch to George and Clara Olmstead Smith. The two sisters donated the Olmstead Ranch to Washington State to become Olmstead State Park. *Image BPC-11-74 by Breckon, Fred L., 1883–1971, courtesy of Ellensburg Library Collection.*

Unfortunately, Mr. Olmstead died just seven years later, but his family continued running the farm, focusing on dairy production. In the early 1900s, the family constructed a bigger home and a barn. Soon, the fascinating convenience of electricity became available, followed by gas-powered tractors, and the family farm was running at full speed with all of the new advances in technology.

The fate of the private family farm would soon become public, as the grandchildren of the Olmsteads, Leta May and Clareta Smith, deeded the entire property to Washington State Parks and Recreation Commission in 1968.

There was only one condition: the farm must remain in its original form and be used as a museum for future generations to enjoy so they could understand the way of pioneer life.

Olmstead Place Historical State Park is a 217-acre day-use park that caters to twenty thousand visitors each year. If you visit, you can enjoy the gardens and antique farm relics. Bring a picnic. The home displays pioneer artifacts such as tools, furniture, clothing, household items, farm implements, and machinery. Olmstead Place Historical State Park is located at 921 Ferguson Road, Ellensburg, WA 98926.

Mel's Mysterious Bottomless Hole
in the Ground

Ellensburg has been known for all kinds of mysteries, from Big Foot sightings to UFO activity. An area called Manastash Ridge supposedly has one of the biggest mysteries of all—Mel's Hole. Not very many people have actually seen the hole, but many legends surround it and its paranormal activity. One local, a Native American shaman (or medicine man) called Red Elk, said his dad first showed him the hole in 1961.

There are claims that it has miraculous healing powers, it can somehow bring dead animals back to life, there is an underground government conspiracy going on—and many other tales.

How deep is this hole? People have claimed to drop a whole reel of fishing line down it and never hit the bottom. That's fifteen miles. On the radio show *Coast to Coast* AM, a nationally syndicated talk show, a guest calling himself Mel Waters claimed the hole exists, yet no such person was listed as resident in that area. Why would he lie?

Other people claim that when they hold a radio near the hole it magically plays old programs from the past no longer on the air.

Geologists who have researched this hole claim it is just an old mining shaft with no powers whatsoever. Located somewhere about ten miles south from Ellensburg, it seems that actual location is hidden. If it were an old mining shaft, then the depth would range from ninety to three hundred feet deep or more.

If people claim this hole is 80,000 feet deep, then that would mean it is deeper than the recorded deepest mine shaft, which is in Russia, 40,230 feet drilled in 1989.

Is Mel's Hole real or just a myth? Stories support both claims. Perhaps someone someday can actually find it?

Central Washington University

Many people claim that the university is haunted. Three halls are rumored to have spirits haunting them: Beck, Kamola and Barto Halls.

Students report seeing apparitions and hearing strange noises in Beck Hall. Kamola Hall is reported to have the spirit of a young female in mourning over the loss of her fiancé, who was tragically killed in World War II. She was so distraught over his untimely death that in 1940 she hanged herself in the attic to ease her sorrow. When Kamola Hall was being remodeled in 2003, her ghostly antics were more prevalent.

Expert paranormal researchers believe that ghostly activity increases during times of construction or remodel, as it can awaken the spirits. Others believe that ghosts don't appreciate things being changed.

People have reported music playing out of nowhere, the knocking and opening and closing of doors, strange sounds and unusual foggy forms in the hallways. The following is reprinted with permission from "Lola in Kamola: CWU's Resident Ghost," by Chelsea Krotzer, October 31, 2009:

Some say she's just the free spirit of a former student, now returned. Others say she committed suicide after discovering the love of her life was killed in action during World War II. What is for certain, is that the story of a "spirit" known as Lola has a legacy that has lived on in Kamola Hall on Central Washington University's Campus for decades. Walking through Kamola's halls Thursday afternoon, one student had written "Lola Kamola was here," on a whiteboard outside their room. Another said they heard stories that a student was awakened by music from their computer that mysteriously started to play by itself. A third just laughed at the idea of a ghost in their hall.

"There's all different kinds of speculation with Lola, how she has arrived or may have arrived at Kamola," said Becky Watson, director of public relations and marketing. "There's (theories) that she just showed up after being gone or she may have committed suicide. No one really knows the true story."

CWU photographer Richard Villacres says he dealt with Lola personally during a photo shoot in 2002, prior to the Kamola Hall remodel. Villacres and a woman modeling a 1940s-era wedding dress made their way up to the attic of Kamola Hall, which in one tale is where the ghost allegedly hanged herself after discovering her fiancé had been killed. During the photo shoot, things seemed fine. Then he developed his film. "I shot three rolls of film inside Kamola of my model, and the three rolls of film that I shot inside—two of them came out black, nothing—which has never, ever happened to me," Villacres said. Getting angered by the apparent camera malfunction, Villacres was surprised to see the third roll of film developed—but not into something that he took.

"The one roll that came out had all kinds of bizarre fogging and weird marks on it," Villacres said. "Especially one photo that was taken in the hallway inside. There is this ghostly figure in the background—all this weird effect is on there. I had no explanation for that." Puzzled and thoroughly creeped out, Villacres had the film sent back to Polaroid to see if there was anything wrong. They said there was nothing. He developed other photos he had taken that day outside the building. They turned out fine. He took his camera out on another shoot, and again, everything was working perfectly. Just not in Kamola's attic.

"She screwed with my film, and, honestly, I have no explanation for it," Villacres said. "Something weird happened."

Barto Hall is believed to be haunted, too. Room C-37 on the top floor of the university is said to be haunted by a young man.

18

HAUNTED THEATERS

LIBERTY THEATRE

There's more than a good time happening at this place. The Liberty Theatre on Fifth Street in Ellensburg has its customers and employees always looking over their shoulders, waiting for an icy hand to touch them. People often claim they hear horrifying late-night screams and witness doors opening and closing by themselves. Ghostly apparitions and noises make this building a little more exciting than just popcorn and a movie.

It is located at 111 East Fifth Avenue in Ellensburg.

CAPITOL THEATRE

Another haunted theater resides on South Third Street in Yakima. The Capital Theatre was built in 1920 by a man named Mercy who dreamed of owning the biggest and best vaudeville theater around. With the invention of movies, the theater transformed from live shows to reels. Over the years, the building suffered, and looming threats of tearing it down began to surface. The townspeople, worried about losing such a beautiful and historic building, bounded together in the hopes of rescuing it. Soon the city purchased the building, but a tragic electrical fire broke out just days later and burned the building to the ground. The theater was painstakingly restored to its original glory—even down to the intricate moldings.

It is believed that the Capitol's stage manager in the 1930s, "Shorty," haunts the theater to this day. Supposedly, the very upset Shorty, torn over the unreturned love of a beautiful actress, took his own life on the theater's stage. Since then, late-night staff have reported eerie activities such as props going missing, objects moving and faint whispers and moans.

It is located at 19 South Third Street in Yakima.

IN CONCLUSION

Stories of ghosts, hauntings and restless spirits have been around as long as living people have been alive, and they will continue until the end of time. Perhaps people are fascinated by them because they want some sort of proof there is life after death; they desire to know their loved ones are not suffering or simply because they are interesting.

As technology advances, the desire to capture proof of their existence has increased dramatically and is no longer limited to Ouija boards, crystal balls, tea leaves, psychics and slate writers. People do not frown upon those who choose to believe in ghosts and the spirit world as much as they did in the past. It is very common to hear conversations about ghosts and spirits almost everywhere you go.

Leavenworth has tugged at people's hearts since its development, and residents continue to love its century-old streets and historic buildings. As locals and visitors roam in and out of the stores, I hope they find these stories from the past intriguing. I also hope this book makes them stop in the entryways of the Tumwater Inn, the old Losekamp Building or any other wonderful store in Leavenworth and the nearby towns and pause for just a second or two to remember those who worked so hard to create the towns everyone loves today.

Who knows, maybe you will even spot or hear a mischievous, friendly ghost or two. Or hopefully (if you desire) you might feel the lightest touch of a hand as a spirit tries to touch the side of your face as you turn to walk away.

Das Auge sieht weit, der Verstand noch weiter.
"The eye looks but it is the mind that sees."

Cascade Bar

Several unidentified men and a dog enjoy posing in front of the Cascade Bar in Leavenworth, which was located on Front Street next to the Leavenworth State Bank. *Courtesy of the* Leavenworth Echo, *September 11, 1914.*

SOURCES

Articles

Becker, Paula. "Prohibition in Washington State." HistoryLink.org, November 20, 2010. http://www.historylink.org/File/9630.

Black Diamond Historical Society. "Franklin: Everything You Always Wanted to Know." February 4, 2011. https://blackdiamondhistory. wordpress.com/2011/02/04/franklin-everything-you-always-wanted-to-know.

Caro, Heather. "Hunting for the Haunted." *Yakima Magazine*, September 10, 2010.

Crotzer, Chelsea. "Lola in Kamola: CWU's Resident Ghost." *Daily Record*, October 31, 2009. http://www.dailyrecordnews.com/news/lola-in-kamola-cwu-s-resident-ghost/article_81f5e264-ff54-592c-a6ad-2220080e4179.html.

New York Times. "84 in Buried Cars; Few Can Be Alive." March 8, 1910.

———. "Fifty Probably Killed." May 11, 1892.

Seattle Press-Times. "J.M. Pinckney." January 10, 1892.

Wenatchee Daily World. "Actor Tells of Wreck at Downs." May 23, 1907.

———. "Engine Plunges into Raging River." June 4, 1907.

SOURCES

Books

Bragg, L.E. *Myths and Mysteries of Washington*. Guilford, CT: TwoDot, 2005.
Kinney-Holck, Rose, and the Upper Valley Museum. Images of America: *Leavenworth*. Mount Pleasant, SC: Arcadia Publishing, 2011.
Martin, Ken, and Vida Martin. *Gold Mining in Washington State*. Stanwood, WA: Golden Treasures Publishing, 1995.

Newspapers

Leavenworth Echo
New York Times
Wenatchee Daily World

Websites

blackpast.org
bricksaloon.com
cashandtreasures.wikifoundry.com
cityofcashmere.org
exploringhistoryinyourhikingboots.com/liberty-ghost-town-wa-usa-1
findagrave.com
ghosttownsofwashington.com
ghosttownsusa.com
hauntedhovel.com/hauntedplacesinwashington.html
historylink.org
nationalgeographic.com
parks.state.wa.us/556/Olmstead-Place
raregoldnuggets.com
treasurenet.com
washingtongold.net
washingtonourhome.com/washington-only-living-ghost-town
westernmininghistory.com
wikipedia.org

Miscellaneous

"Roslyn Mine Disaster (October 3, 1909): The Official Investigative Report of the Washington State Inspector of Coal Mines." Information from the official report by State Inspector Botting, December 31, 1910. http://www.historylink.org/File/9182.

Skykomish Historical Society. "A Walking Tour of Historic Skykomish." www.skykomishhotel.com/skykomish-hotel-history.

Waters, Mel. "Art Bell: Somewhere in Time." Coast to Coast AM, October 22, 2011. www.coasttocoastam.com/guest/waters-mel/5595.

ABOUT THE AUTHOR

Originally from Upstate New York, Deborah Cuyle now lives in Snohomish, Washington, and loves everything about small towns. She has written three other books: *Kidding Around Portland, Oregon*; *Cannon Beach, Oregon*; and *Haunted Snohomish, Washington*. Her passions include local history, animals, the beach, art and writing. Her historic Snohomish farm is home to multiple rescued animals, including a grouchy three-legged cat and a pony named Minnie Winnie Butterball. She also provides a horsemanship program to Girl Scouts. Deborah enjoys thinking about the possibility of an afterlife and especially loves telling a chilling ghost story while nestled beside a bonfire with her best friends and family.

Visit us at
www.historypress.net
....
This title is also available as an e-book